CONTENTS

FOREWORD

To facilitate accountable and high quality professional work, the Division of Educational and Child Psychology of The British Psychological Society convened a Working Party to consider the assessment of dyslexia. The Working Party met for the first time in February 1998 to undertake a three-stage process of investigation and reporting consisting of the following tasks:

✦ To consider relevant research and to survey current practice in order to write a relatively brief draft report that focuses on the assessment of school-aged children.

✦ To circulate the draft report as widely as possible in order to obtain responses from researchers with expertise in this field, educational psychology services, individual educational psychologists with an interest in the topic, course tutors and other relevant professionals.

✦ To revise the report in the light of the consultation and then publish a document that makes recommendations about the concept of dyslexia and the principles of educational psychology assessment relating to this concept.

The present report represents the completion of the work. As shown in the account of the consultation that took place (see Appendix B), the report has the support of practising educational psychologists and leading academic researchers in this field. Section 2 presents a working definition of dyslexia that provides the unifying thread throughout all sections of the report. Section 3 outlines relevant literacy research, Section 4 describes different theoretical explanations, and Sections 5 and 6 consider implications for educational psychology assessment and intervention in the context of current educational policy. As the intention is to provide a coherent and logical account, it is strongly recommended that the report be read in its entirety. Isolated quotes may misrepresent the report.

The Working Party would like to express its gratitude to all those who responded to the consultation and assisted with the writing and revising of the report. Their names and/or organisations are listed in the acknowledgements section.

Although the report has been ratified by the Committee of the Division of Educational and Child Psychology of The British Psychological Society, responsibility for it remains with the Working Party, comprising the following members:

Rea Reason, University of Manchester and Oldham Educational Psychology Service (Chair);

Norah Frederickson, University College London and Buckinghamshire Educational Psychology Service;

Maria Heffernan, Manchester Educational Psychology Service (Representing the National Association of Principal Educational Psychologists);

Conrad Martin, Gateshead Educational Psychology Service (Representing the Association of Educational Psychologists);

Kevin Woods, University of Manchester and Rochdale Educational Psychology Service.

SUMMARY

1. This report considers the concept of dyslexia in the context of current research in the area of literacy learning in general and the difficulties that can arise in the development of word reading and spelling skills. Key Stages 1 and 2 within the National Curriculum in the UK (children aged about 5 to 11 years) are its primary focus but the report has implications beyond this age range. The report is based on extensive consultation with practising educational psychologists and leading academic researchers in this field. It provides an illustration of the way educational psychology considers practice in relation to theory and research.

2. Following a similar enquiry in the Netherlands, the report adopts a working definition of dyslexia that separates description from causal explanations. The working definition is as follows: *Dyslexia is evident when accurate and fluent word reading and/or spelling develops very incompletely or with great difficulty. This focuses on literacy learning at the 'word level' and implies that the problem is severe and persistent despite appropriate learning opportunities. It provides the basis for a staged process of assessment through teaching.*

3. The report gives full recognition to the plight of learners with difficulties of a dyslexic nature. These difficulties can act as barriers to educational, social and vocational opportunities. Whatever the debates about this phenomenon and its associated terminology, the report is intended to further positive and constructive ways of helping these children.

4. The working definition provides a unifying thread throughout all sections of the report. It is the starting point for an outline of relevant literacy research and for the evaluation of different theoretical explanations. These two sections, in turn, lead to the consideration of the working definition as it applies to educational psychology assessment and intervention and in the context of current educational policy regarding the concept of special educational needs.

5. A review of relevant literacy research points to the cognitive processes and instructional circumstances that are most likely to lead to successful learning of word recognition and spelling. The converging view of the central role of phonology in both skilled reading and in accounts of how children become skilled readers, would suggest that weaknesses in phonological processing and representational abilities are highly likely to affect the learner's word reading and spelling development. Within this context, dyslexia becomes a function of the reciprocal effects of learning opportunities and the type and extent of phonological and semantic strengths and weaknesses.

6. The report considers theoretical explanations within a causal modelling framework involving three levels of analysis: the biological (brain), the cognitive and the behavioural. Some of the theoretical accounts of dyslexia include comprehensive description at each level in the framework and, in addition, model causal links between the features included at different levels. The phonological deficit/delay hypothesis provides the main focus, both because of the broad empirical support that it commands and because of the role phonology is accorded in many of the other hypotheses in mediating the impact of dyslexia on the acquisition of word reading and spelling skills. It is important to consider, however, the extent to which available empirical evidence suggests that different theories should be regarded as alternative accounts of a unitary construct of 'dyslexia', as opposed to being regarded as accounts of different types of dyslexia.

7. The working definition adopted in this report requires that three aspects be evaluated through the assessment process. First, assessment needs to consider whether the pupil is learning/has learnt accurate and fluent word reading and/or spelling very incompletely, second, whether appropriate learning opportunities have been provided and, third, whether progress has been made only as a result of much additional effort/instruction and that difficulties have, nevertheless, persisted. The report considers the steps that educational psychologists, together with teachers, parents and the learners themselves, can take to collect assessment information in relation to each of these elements.

8. The conclusion that the acquisition of reading and spelling is 'very incomplete' depends on the age and developmental stage of the learner. It triggers an investigation of factors that may be important in understanding the nature of the difficulties being experienced and in identifying ways of overcoming or alleviating them. The assessment builds on publications that provide guidance for educational psychology work in general, such as the DECP framework for psychological assessment and intervention (see Appendix D), and emphasises the multifaceted nature of that work. Not only are individual and instructional variables taken into account, but also social, motivational and organisational ones.

9. During the consultation phase of this report, researchers and practitioners both identified the evaluation of persistence as a central issue that needed further development. In the present revised report, research regarding the effectiveness of learning opportunities in the classroom relating, in particular, to learning within the National Literacy Strategy provide the overall context. The evaluation of persistence in the light of response to additional teaching can then involve the monitoring of rate of learning progress through methods such as single-subject experimental research and precision teaching. These methods offer a set of strategies for carrying out focused assessments of pupil performance over time and for recording progress in a way that facilitates judgements about accuracy and fluency of performance. Further work is needed in this area.

10. The identification/explanation of dyslexia and the assessment/determination of special educational needs are two separate issues. Within educational legislation in the UK, the continuum of special educational needs is defined in relation to special educational provision. It allows for variation in the manifestation of special educational needs since what provision is considered to be special may vary between teachers, schools and local education authorities. Consequently, local policy largely determines cut-off points for special educational provision regarding the continuum of mild/moderate/severe levels of dyslexia. Nevertheless, the working definition adopted in this report can provide a starting point for social policy decisions. The features of the definition (severity, persistence) may, along with other relevant indicators, inform judgements at the local education authority level regarding severe and long-term special educational needs.

11. The concept of special educational needs provides the rationale for the assessment of other difficulties that may be associated with dyslexia and the determination of learning support that enables access to appropriate areas of the curriculum. Information can be obtained from an overview of the child's curriculum and programmes of study as well as from more direct observations that test out hypotheses about modes of curriculum presentation and learner response.

12. In the present report dyslexia is regarded primarily as a mainstream educational issue. This implies that educational psychologists work with schools to develop effective school-based assessment, intervention and monitoring and, within that context, also carry out

detailed psychological assessment and programme planning to promote the progress of those children whose difficulties are most severe and persistent.

13. With regard to early identification, educational psychologists can help teachers and carers to *notice* children's individual needs and then adjust their responses accordingly. Given the tools for interactive assessment and teaching that can be included in the Early Years Curriculum and the Reception Year of the National Literacy Strategy, it is possible to monitor progress in early literacy learning and to notice which children continue to need help.

14. Culture-fair assessment requires that learning difficulties of a dyslexic nature are identified across languages, cultures, socio-economic status, race and gender. Even when the learner's home language is not English, research has shown that phonological difficulties, as one of the important determinants of literacy, can be identified in the language of tuition. The purpose is then to piece together the puzzle of dyslexia within a particular educational, social and cultural context. This involves an understanding of the literacy learning process and the reciprocal effects of educational achievements, cognitive processes, instructional circumstances and the learner's perceptions, strategies and experiences. To be useful, the assessment needs to lead to workable plans of action.

RECOMMENDATIONS

THE CONCEPT OF DYSLEXIA

It is recommended that:

1. Research and practice acknowledges the working definition of dyslexia introduced in this report which separates description from causal explanations. (The working definition states that *dyslexia is evident when accurate and fluent word reading and/or spelling develops very incompletely or with great difficulty. This focuses on literacy learning at the 'word level' and implies that the problem is severe and persistent despite appropriate learning opportunities. It provides the basis for a staged process of assessment through teaching.*)

2. The working definition provides a starting point for considering relevant research about literacy learning and different theoretical explanations of dyslexia which current stressing the central role of literacy-related phonological skills.

3. Learning difficulties of a dyslexic nature are recognised across languages, culture, race, socio-economic status and gender.

ASSESSMENT AND INTERVENTION

It is recommended that:

4. Assessment and intervention is considered in the context of overall learning opportunities and, in particular, the learning opportunities offered by the National Curriculum and the National Literacy Strategy in the UK.

5. Psychological assessment and intervention is regarded within a general psychological framework, such as that published by the DECP, where educational psychologists work together with pupils, parents/carers and teachers in evaluating the interaction between individual, instructional, social and organisational variables.

6. Educational psychology assessment and intervention is based on research about children's acquisition of literacy. The assessment can take into account the reciprocal effects of learning opportunities and the type and extent of phonological, orthographic, and semantic strengths and difficulties and include, when appropriate, evaluation of any associated learning difficulties and emotional consequences.

7. Identification/explanation of dyslexia is regarded as conceptually separate from the assessment/determination of special educational needs. While the former draws on cognitive research and theory, the latter depends primarily on issues relating to social policy concerned with the effects of learning difficulties. In considering severity and persistence of learning difficulties, both can start from the present working definition.

8. Dyslexia is regarded primarily as a mainstream educational issue involving a continuum of assistance as determined by the severity and persistence of word reading and spelling difficulties.

RESEARCH AND DEVELOPMENT

It is recommended that:

9. As part of initial training and continuing professional development, educational psychologists keep up-to-date with and contribute to developments in literacy research and practice.

10. Educational psychologists work together with teachers and parents/carers to develop approaches and skills so that individual needs can be noticed from an early stage and teaching adjusted to accommodate these needs.

11. Further research is initiated to:

✦ develop methods for assessing severity and persistence, such as curriculum-related measures of reading and spelling and techniques for monitoring rates of progress in response to intervention over time;

✦ develop and evaluate instructional approaches and interventions in order to create an evidence base on the effectiveness of approaches relevant to dyslexia;

✦ use the working definition as the basis for clarifying the range of possible causes and associated behavioural and/or cognitive features of dyslexia.

Section 1: INTRODUCTION

1.1   IN SEARCH OF A LITMUS TEST OF DYSLEXIA

In order to ascertain whether the term 'acid' applies to a given liquid, insert a strip of blue litmus paper into it; the liquid is an acid if and only if the litmus paper turns red.
(Hempel, 1966)

The scientific basis of psychology requires precise operational definitions of the meanings of the terms used. Without such operational definitions, there can be little objective comparison of different observations, let alone debate about different explanations of the observations made. In this light, definitions of dyslexia should be sufficiently clear to enable practitioners to assess whether and to what extent individuals can be described by this term. The need for approximations of the litmus test is thus evident, not only for scientific and educational reasons, but also to enable psychologists to explain their practices in a society that expects them to have such litmus tests. For this reason, it is important that educational psychologists come to a working agreement about the concept of dyslexia and its assessment.

1.2   THE REMIT OF THE WORKING PARTY

To facilitate accountable and high quality assessment, the Division of Educational and Child Psychology of The British Psychological Society convened a Working Party consisting of five educational psychologists with recognised expertise in this field of applied practice and dyslexia. The group included representation from the Association of Educational Psychologists and the National Association of Principal Educational Psychologists. The remit of the Working Party was to review relevant research and practice in order to write a brief report to clarify the current concept of dyslexia, its links with literacy learning/difficulties and implications for educational psychology assessments. School-aged children were to be the primary focus of the report.

The Working Party met for the first time in February 1998 to undertake a three-stage process of investigation and reporting consisting of the following tasks:

1. To consider relevant research and to survey current practice in order to write a relatively brief draft report.

2. To circulate the draft report as widely as possible in order to obtain responses from researchers with expertise in this field, educational psychology services, individual educational psychologists with an interest in the topic, course tutors and other relevant professionals.

3. To revise the report in the light of the consultation and then publish a document that makes recommendations about the concept of dyslexia and the principles of educational psychology assessment relating to this concept.

1.3   A SURVEY OF EDUCATIONAL PSYCHOLOGY PRACTICE

To gain a picture of current practices and to enable the report to respond to issues identified by practitioners as important, a questionnaire was circulated to LEA educational psychology services in March 1998. Sixty services provided information about assessment policies related to specific learning difficulties/dyslexia, examples of documentation and the provision being made. The data is presented in Appendix A and relevant sections of the main report refer to this information. The areas that respondents wished the working party to consider can be grouped under five main headings:

✦ to clarify the concept/definition/models of specific learning difficulties (dyslexia);

✦ to outline approaches to assessment and models of assessment;

✦ to discuss assessment in the context of intervention;

✦ to consider the implications arising from the relativity of the concepts of dyslexia and special educational needs;

✦ to facilitate a consistent approach that has sufficient flexibility to incorporate all valid paradigms of psychological assessment.

The report incorporates responses to these issues in as far as its remit has permitted. More comprehensive considerations of aspects such as methods of intervention will have to be addressed elsewhere.

1.4   CONSULTATION BASED ON THE DRAFT REPORT

In January 1999 a draft report was circulated for consultation to all educational psychology services, members of the DECP, course tutors, researchers with expertise in this field and others with a particular interest in the topic. The total number of responses received was 214 and, of these, 141 were from practising educational psychologists in 84 local authority services in England, Wales and Northern Ireland. Many of the responses were representative of the collective views of the services.

Appendix B outlines the results of the consultation and shows that the draft report has the support of the vast majority of respondents. With regard to the term 'dyslexia' there is concern by some about the use of terminology that implies too narrow a focus on within-child causative factors rather than effective teaching and inclusive practices. Conversely, the emphasis in the report on dyslexia as a mainstream issue worries those who fear that serious problems could be overlooked. Those wishing to avoid the term suggest synonyms such as 'literacy difficulties', 'persistent and severe literacy difficulties' and 'learning difficulties in literacy'. With this caveat, the respondents agree with much of the content of the report. A substantial majority acknowledge that debate about the use of the term 'dyslexia' is counterproductive. Particularly high agreement is achieved in relation to the following aspects covered in the report:

✦ the use of a working definition of dyslexia that separates description from causal explanations;

✦ the analysis of children's reading and spelling performance in the context of their instructional experiences;

✦ the evaluation of interactive explanations in the light of different hypotheses of dyslexia;

✦ the consideration of dyslexia within the DECP framework for psychological assessment and intervention in general;

- the recognition of dyslexia as a mainstream educational issue;

- the application of the working definition in social policy decisions;

- the importance of keeping up to date with developments in literacy research and practice.

The report provides an example of the way educational psychologists consider practice in relation to cognitive theory and research. In the light of the working definition adopted by the report, both educational practitioners and academic researchers highlighted the need to give greater consideration to the persistence of difficulties despite appropriate learning opportunities.

1.5   THE RATIONALE AND STRUCTURE OF THE REPORT

The present report builds on a previous national enquiry commissioned by the Division of Educational and Child Psychology of the British Psychological Society entitled *Specific Learning Difficulties (Dyslexia): Challenges and Responses* (Pumfrey & Reason, 1991). It also links with the *Code of Practice on the identification and assessment of special educational need* (DfEE, 1994) and the subsequent *Green Paper* (DfEE, 1997). It is designed to complement the guidance for educational psychology statutory assessments (AEP, 1998) and the guidance for educational psychology assessments in general (DECP, 1999) reproduced in Appendix D of this report. It is in full accordance with the British Psychological Society Code of Conduct for Psychologists which states that the profession of psychology *'shall value integrity, impartiality and respect for persons and evidence and shall seek to establish the highest ethical standards in their work'* (The BPS 1994, p.1). The promotion of fair and evidence-based practice is central to this endeavour.

The structure of the report reflects the process of scientific enquiry adopted by the working party. In the second section, a discussion of the concept of dyslexia leads to a working definition without explanatory elements. The third section considers dyslexia in the context of skilled reading and spelling and concludes that assessment involves, in the first instance, analysis of the child's reading and spelling performance and learning experiences. The fourth section explores different theoretical explanations that can account for the working definition within a causal modelling framework. The fifth section considers implications for educational psychology assessment and intervention. The sixth section discusses the concept of special educational needs in the light of the information provided in the previous sections. The final section draws together the conclusions from all the sections of the report.

1.6   CONCLUSIONS

- The present report is based on reviews of relevant research, a survey of current educational psychology practice and extensive consultation based on a draft report.

- The report builds on a previous national enquiry instigated by the DECP and is designed to complement the DECP guidance for educational psychology assessment in general. It is in full accordance with The British Psychological Society Code of Conduct for Psychologists.

- The report considers the concept of dyslexia in relation to relevant educational legislation and links with the Code of Practice on the identification and assessment of special educational need (DfEE, 1994) and the subsequent Green Paper (DfEE, 1997).

Section 2: A WORKING DEFINITION OF DYSLEXIA

2.1   THE WIDER CULTURAL CONTEXT

An entitlement to literacy is considered a basic human right and so reflects the central role of reading and writing in all societies (United Nations resolutions 45/199 and 50/143). In this country the Year of Reading, which started in September 1998, underlined the social and political importance given to the ability to communicate in written form. These developments provide the backdrop for public debate about literacy.

On the basis of their experiences, the public may formulate its own theories about the acquisition of literacy and its own explanations for individual failure to do so. The term 'dyslexia' does not therefore belong to cognitive psychology or education alone. As described by Woods (1998), it has entered the realms of popular language and requires consideration from an additional social psychological standpoint. Even today there may be perceived links between reading ability, privilege and intelligence that have their roots in our educational and social history. The absolute labels of 'dyslexia' or 'intelligence' can then serve to simplify complexities and relativities. Public perception may see the weaker literacy skills of intelligent children from well-educated homes as more unexpected and intriguing than those of other struggling readers (Stanovich, 1996). MacKay (1999) argues that such assumptions can raise fundamental issues regarding equality of opportunity. As educational psychologists work in contexts circumscribed by social policy (see Section 6), views based on 'folk psychology' are likely to impact on their practice.

2.2   THE CONCEPT OF DYSLEXIA

The word 'dyslexia' has been, and continues to be, the focus and stimulus for considerable research activity and debate within the disciplines of psychology, education and medicine. In cognitive psychology, dyslexia has for many years been a short-hand for marked difficulty with the alphabetic script. As such, it has generated a substantial body of empirical research leading to theoretical debate about the sources and explanations of these difficulties. However, meaningful resolutions about conceptualisation and identification across all spheres of involvement have not been reached (Rutter, 1998). The term has often been avoided in educational practice because of its predominant emphasis on within child causative factors and its perceived effects on social policy, i.e. the risk of unequal distribution of limited public resources.

Following considerable debate in the 1970s and 80s (for a review see Pumfrey & Reason, 1991), when many practitioners expressed serious reservations about the concept, education in the UK opted for the term 'specific learning difficulties' while similar developments in the US resulted in 'learning disabilities' or 'specific learning disability'. With the continued use of 'dyslexia' in cognitive research and in psycho-medical practice, the Code of Practice (DfEE, 1994) subsequently chose the compromise phrase 'specific learning difficulties (for example dyslexia)' while on page 15 the Green Paper refers to 'children with

16

specific learning difficulties (such as dyslexia)' (DfEE, 1997). Legal precedents have also established the existence of 'dyslexia' in law (see Chasty & Friel, 1991). Simultaneously, as discussed in section 2.1, 'dyslexia ' now appears to be well embedded in popular language and often used synonymously with 'specific learning difficulties' in professional practice.

2.3   ACQUIRED VS. DEVELOPMENTAL DYSLEXIA

One area of research has examined adult patients who, due to known neurological damage caused by a stroke, traffic accident or tumour, have lost their ability to read and write. With the co-operation of these adults, attempts have been made to map the brain areas affected to particular skill deficits, including those that involve a lack of understanding of the meanings of words that the patients can read. This neuro-psychological information is of considerable importance in cognitive research.

It is essential, however, to distinguish between research with adults who have 'acquired' dyslexia and research with children who have not developed adequate literacy skills in the first place (Karmiloff-Smith, 1997). Results from the former do not tell us how young children learn to read or fail to learn to read, although similarities in theoretical models have been noted (see Section 3.7). As parallels must not be drawn too easily between the two distinct areas of concern, Pumfrey (1996) prefers the exact term 'specific developmental dyslexia' (SDD). However, as discussed in Sections 2.1 and 2.2, everyday use now tends to refer to 'dyslexia' as a learning difficulty when there is no known neurological damage relevant to the acquisition of reading and writing skills. That is the focus of the present report.

2.4   DYSLEXIA AND SCIENTIFIC ENQUIRY

'When I use the word,' Humpty Dumpty said …, 'it means just what I choose it to mean – neither more or less.'
'The question is,' said Alice, 'whether you can make words mean so many different things.'
'The question is,' said Humpty Dumpty, 'which is to be the master – that's all.'
(Carroll, 1872, *Through the Looking Glass*)

For a word to be used as a scientific concept, it must satisfy certain criteria. Stanovich (1996) proposes that a well-defined biologically based condition should have distinct phenotypic (performance) patterns, distinct heritability patterns and distinct neuro-anatomical characteristics. Similarly Pumfrey and Reason (op. cit.) state that the existence and labelling of a condition requires that it should satisfy one or more of the following criteria: it should have distinct aetiology, identifying characteristics, prognosis and response to intervention. Currently dyslexia does not meet such stringent requirements. Much research is in progress on aspects of heredity (Pennington, 1990; Scarborough, 1991; Lyytinen, 1997), neuro-anatomical characteristics and brain scans (Galaburda, 1989; Eden *et al.*, 1996; Frith, 1997) and, as considered in Section 4, different theoretical standpoints may emphasise different performance patterns of dyslexia.

Tyler (1990) and more recently Tonnessen (1997) point to the varieties of terminology and fuzzy definitions as major sources of disparate findings concerning the extent and causes of dyslexia. According to Tonnessen, the search for clear and consistent terminology is in itself a useful primary task of scientific investigation. Tonnessen's argument for an operational definition, without explanatory elements, gains support from Elaine Miles (1995), who considers it impossible to provide one authoritative theoretical definition since dyslexia is too multifaceted and complex to be defined in terms of any single theoretical stance.

2.5   A WORKING DEFINITION OF DYSLEXIA

Etymologically, the term dyslexia is derived from two Greek words – 'dys' meaning 'difficulty' and 'lexis' meaning 'words'. The literal meaning of dyslexia is thus 'difficulty with words' which may be extrapolated to 'difficulty with reading and spelling words'. At this level of analysis there need be no casual explanation.

A Committee of the Health Council of the Netherlands has prepared a report on the definition and treatment of dyslexia (Gersons-Wolfensberger & Ruijssenaars, 1997). The committee considers that a working definition of dyslexia should fulfil the following conditions:

✦ the definition should be descriptive with no explanatory elements;

✦ the definition should be specific enough to identify dyslexia within the whole of severe reading and spelling problems;

✦ the definition should be general enough to allow for various scientific explanatory models and any developments those models might undergo;

✦ the definition should be operationalisable for the purposes of research;

✦ the definition should be directive for statements concerning the need for intervention and applicable to the various groups involved.

On this basis the Committee of the Health Council of the Netherlands arrived at the following working definition of dyslexia:

Dyslexia is present when the automatization of word identification (reading) and/or word spelling does not develop or does so very incompletely or with great difficulty (p.209).

The term automatization refers here to a reading and writing style characterised by a high level of speed and accuracy requiring little conscious attention. As the process is 'difficult to suppress, ignore or influence', it contrasts starkly with the deliberate, laborious and inaccurate approach adopted by those who struggle with basic literacy.

The Dutch working definition seems appropriate for our purposes. However, the word 'automatization' may be confusing in the UK context as it is also used in causal explanations based on the skills automatization hypothesis (see Section 4.6 in this report). It seems clearer, therefore, to substitute this term with a phrase referring to fluency and accuracy. Our proposed working definition is shown in Table 2.1.

TABLE 2.1: A WORKING DEFINITION OF DYSLEXIA

Dyslexia is evident when accurate and fluent word reading and/or spelling develops very incompletely or with great difficulty. This focuses on literacy learning at the 'word level' and implies that the problem is severe and persistent despite appropriate learning opportunities. It provides the basis for a staged process of assessment through teaching.

In terms of the National Literacy Strategy (DfEE, 1998), dyslexia can be defined as marked and persistent problems at the word level of the NLS curricular framework. As such, it links with the evaluation of learning opportunities and teaching methods as mainstream educational issues (see sections 5 and 6). Furthermore, the working definition provides a starting point for assessing the extent to which the literacy difficulties are leading to special educational needs that hinder appropriate access to relevant areas of the curriculum. In terms of the Code of Practice (DfEE, 1994), and its revision under consultation at the time of writing, the working definition accords with the staged process of assessment through teaching central to the Code.

It needs to be noted, however, that this is a working definition, not an operational definition. It does not resolve issues of deciding how long to wait before considering that accurate/fluent word reading and/or spelling is developing 'very incompletely' and 'with great difficulty'. These judgements differ at successive developmental stages and require quantification of the amount of instructional effort involved. Cut-off points within a continuum of special educational needs and provision remain a thorny issue (See sections 6.1 and 6.2). Nevertheless, as discussed in Section 6.5, the working definition can also clarify decision making at a social policy level.

The advantage of the present definition is that it can accommodate different theoretical explanations to be considered in Section 4 in relation to the causal modelling framework, introduced by Morton and Frith (1995), with its three levels of observation and explanation: the biological, the cognitive and the behavioural. Although within-child constitutional factors are afforded a central place, environmental factors play a key role at all levels of explanation. Educational practitioners place particular emphasis on environmental factors because the environment is currently the source of intervention and management efforts.

The present working definition can be regarded as 'proximal' (see Section 5.2). It provides a starting point for generating and testing a broad range of hypotheses that draw on psychological theory and research linked to different causal explanations. At the individual level, this approach encompasses multivariate explanations rather than a search for single causative factors.

2.6   IS 'DYSLEXIA' SYNONYMOUS WITH 'SPECIFIC LEARNING DIFFICULTIES'?

The present working definition has no exclusionary criteria. Pupils with moderate learning difficulties or sensory impairments can also be described as dyslexic if they cannot read (Greaney & Reason, 1999). Positive identifying characteristics focus in the first instance on severe and persistent problems with accurate/fluent word recognition and spelling, and take priority over other factors including linguistic and cultural background.

By definition, the term 'specific learning difficulties' assumes that the literacy problem is in some way 'specific', i.e. that it contrasts with other areas of strength in academic achievement or cognitive development. Whereas 'dyslexia' looks for causal explanations, albeit controversial (see Section 4), 'specific learning difficulties' have traditionally been linked with exclusionary criteria.

Turner (1997) has proposed a rather different distinction suggesting that dyslexia can be considered a subset within the range of different specific learning difficulties that includes autism and ADHD. Only some areas of functioning are affected in each condition.

Historically, the main difference between 'dyslexia' and 'specific learning difficulties' has been in their implied approaches to identification and assessment. Dyslexia has tended to refer to the diagnosis of a condition through symptoms and signs while users of the term 'specific learning difficulties' have focused on a functional analysis of what specifically learners can or cannot do in relation to the tasks of reading and writing and other associated difficulties. From a historical perspective, therefore, the two terms are not synonymous but, if the working definition outlined above is adopted, 'specific learning difficulties' can sit more comfortably with 'dyslexia'.

2.7 CONCLUSIONS

✦ In cognitive psychology 'dyslexia' has for many years been a short-hand for marked difficulty with the alphabetic script. The term has now entered the realms of popular language and also requires consideration from a social psychological standpoint.

✦ Reference to 'dyslexia' has been avoided in educational practice because of its predominant emphasis on within-child causative factors rather than effective teaching and inclusive practices.

✦ A distinction needs to be made between research with adults who have 'acquired' dyslexia due to neurological damage and research with children who have failed to develop adequate literacy skills.

✦ Varieties of terminology and definitions are a major source of disparate findings regarding the extent and causes of dyslexia. To clarify the concept of dyslexia, we need to start with a working definition that separates description from causal explanations.

✦ The following working definition is adopted in the present report: *Dyslexia is evident when accurate and fluent word reading and/or spelling develops very incompletely or with great difficulty. This focuses on literacy learning at the 'word level' and implies that the problem is severe and persistent despite appropriate learning opportunities. It provides the basis for a staged process of assessment through teaching.*

✦ In terms of the National Literacy Strategy (DfEE, 1998), dyslexia can be defined as marked and persistent problems at the word level of the NLS curricular framework. As such, it links with the evaluation of learning opportunities and teaching methods introduced within a mainstream educational setting.

✦ The working definition provides a starting point for generating and testing a broad range of hypotheses that draw on psychological theory and research linked to different causal explanations. At the individual level, this approach encompasses multivariate explanations rather than a search for single causative factors.

✦ The working definition has no exclusionary criteria. Positive identifying characteristics involve in the first instance severe and persistent problems with accurate/fluent word recognition and spelling, and take priority over other factors including linguistic and cultural background.

✦ In focusing on the quantification and understanding of literacy difficulties, the working definition is not synonymous with specific learning difficulties. Nevertheless, it can also provide a starting point for assessing the extent to which literacy difficulties are leading to special educational needs that hinder appropriate access to relevant areas of the curriculum.

Section 3: LITERACY LEARNING AND DYSLEXIA

3.1   INTRODUCTION

Consideration of difficulties in learning to read and spell should be set in the context of our knowledge of skilled performance and of the way that literacy skills are acquired by young learners. This section sets out to summarise some aspects of what is now known about the processes involved in reading and to outline models of skilled performance and their implications for the way in which children learn to become literate. Throughout, references are made to review articles and edited books to enable those interested in the field to undertake further reading.

3.2   THE REGULARITY OF ENGLISH IN READING AND SPELLING

Skilled readers have little difficulty with pronunciation of non-words such as *nordles, nordless, interfascicular.* The addition of *s* to *nordles* immediately and automatically changes the emphasis and break of the new letter string *nordless* (aided no doubt by knowledge of the morpheme *less*). Similarly, skilled readers almost invariably read the first c in *interfascicular* as a soft sound whilst the second c is hard.

The regularity of English print-sound correspondences is important in probabilistic terms. Crossword solvers know how even a few letters narrow down the possibilities. Thus: *r***h generates, from an 88,000 word thesaurus, only 21 words, of which 16 end in ch, 7 end in nch and 10 begin with b or c. Similarly, many word letter-strings are easily decodable without the vowels being identified, e.g. *Nnsns* or *dffdl* (Adams, 1990). These examples demonstrate that skilled word reading involves rapid and automatic mapping of letter strings onto the most likely pronunciation. Skilled spelling also involves an implicit knowledge of the probabilities of particular letter patterns occurring together (see Hulme & Joshi, 1998; Perfetti, Rieben & Fayol, 1997; Treiman, 1998).

3.3   ORTHOGRAPHIC PROCESSING

Smooth and rapid reading gives the impression that very little detailed processing of individual words is involved. In fact, nearly all the words in text are individually processed. Rarely are words skipped, and these tend to be short function words. Up to seven or eight 'bits' are subject to focused (foveal) fixation (Balota & Rayner, 1991; Rayner & Morris, 1992; Irwin, 1998). When words are longer than seven or eight letters, there are few possibilities for the actual word and thus the succeeding fixation may well be shorter. Changes of font type, between or within words, make negligible difference to the speed at which they are read. This research demonstrates that skilled readers are not reading words or letters as pictures but, rapidly and automatically, they are processing the elements within them (for detailed reviews see Adams,1990; Besner & Humphries, 1991; Willows, Kruk & Corcos, 1993).

Also relevant to reading is what affects letter or word information in the parafovea (at the boundaries of the fovea). Significantly, orthographic priming effects of letter information in the parafovea are strengthened when there is a phonological prime (for instance a word that shares the pronunciation with the actual target word such as *pair* and *pear*). Semantic or lexical primes have negligible or no influence on subsequent lexical processes via the fovea (Balota & Rayner, 1991; Pollatsek *et al.*, 1992). In short, the evidence is that there is no lexical pre-priming involved in orthographic processing of print, but there are phonological effects.

Whether, and to what extent, words can be read without recourse to phonology is not completely resolved and needs to be clarified. One view, compatible with the research, is that the role of orthography is to provide some sort of checking procedure to aid phonological and contextual processing. This might explain why dyslexic readers with poor phonological skills tend to show relatively better orthographic skills in reading tasks (Hanley, Reynolds and Thornton 1997; Siegel, Share & Geva 1995).

3.4   PHONOLOGICAL PROCESSING

The speech and language abilities and phonological competencies of young pre-reading children can predict their subsequent reading development (for reviews see Adams, 1990; Blachman, 1998; Hulme & Joshi, 1998; Snowling & Stackhouse, 1996; Stackhouse & Wells, 1997; Stothard, Snowling, Bishop, Chipchase & Kaplan, 1998). The interactions between different facets of early language development are complex and, in terms of predicting later literacy, vary with age and stage of development (Rego & Bryant, 1993; Lazo, Pumfrey & Peers, 1997; Gibbs, 1998).

At least some degree of phonological mediation or processing now appears obligatory in reading (Gough, Ehri & Treiman, 1992; Greaney, Tunmer & Chapman, 1997; Hoien, Lundberg, Stanovich & Bjaalid, 1995; Share & Stanovich, 1995; Share, 1995). It would seem that phonological coding provides a central unifying thread in the word reading process. Even with the pictograms of Chinese script there is evidence of prior phonological activation (Perfetti & Zhang, 1995; Tan, Hoosain & Siok, 1996). The role, amount and relative weight of phonological processing, however, and how complete this has to be, is likely to alter in the course of reading development and developing reading (Snowling, 1998b).

3.5   THE INTERACTION BETWEEN ORTHOGRAPHY, PHONOLOGY AND LANGUAGE CONTEXT

Skilled and fluent readers make little use of contextual clues when word reading other than to clarify the intended meaning when the same spelling has more than one possible meaning, for example in *calf* (part of the leg or an animal), *tear* (cry or rip), *rose* (flower or the past tense for rising). Additionally, for content words like these, accessing the correct pronunciation appears necessary in order to access the correct meaning (Folk & Morris, 1995; Van Orden, 1991). Unlike fluent readers, poor readers require contextual information as an important compensatory strategy in assisting word recognition (Stanovich, 1986; Share, 1995). Once the decoding of initial reading acquisition is established, semantic, syntactic and contextual information are central to the identification of unfamiliar or new printed words in text (Share, 1995) and to reading comprehension (Cain & Oakhill, 1998; Oakhill, Cain & Yuill, 1998; Roth *et al.*, 1996).

Taking all that we know about these reading processes, it is clear that the processes are interactive, priming, constraining, exciting and inhibiting each other as words and text are read. The essence of skilled word reading lies in the ability of the reader to map letter strings on to their most probable pronunciation rapidly and automatically, constrained by word-knowledge (the lexicon), meaning and context, which can deal with exceptions to probability.

3.6   HOW CHILDREN LEARN TO READ AND SPELL

Whole language models of reading and writing development argue that literacy is essentially an extension of language development. In the 1970s such models had enthusiastic advocates (Smith, 1973; Goodman & Goodman, 1977). These models continue to play a central role in stressing that the learning of decoding skills is not meaningful if learners lack an interest in the very purpose of communicating ideas and thoughts through the printed text.

The whole language model describes word reading as a 'psycho-linguistic guessing game'. Driven by a search for meaning, the reader makes educated guesses and anticipates the next words on the basis of the text already read. If rapid visual perception of the word-features confirms the guess, then the reader moves on. A crucial assumption is that most words can be 'read' as wholes, visually. Given the speed and facility shown by skilled readers, the account has a certain intuitive appeal. As shown in previous sections, however, the evidence against such an account of reading behaviour is now incontrovertible. The proposal that reading is accomplished through a combination of cueing strategies, for which learners may have a preference, deflects from the centrality of word decoding in the reading process. Accurate and fluent word decoding may be better regarded as the fundamental sub-skill required for efficient reading for interest and information. The observations that led Smith and Goodman to their view, and the insights into the importance of syntax, semantics and other language issues, must be accounted for, nevertheless, in any model of word reading development.

Stage models of the development of word reading and spelling have not only attracted research interest but also received much attention from educational practitioners (for reviews see Rack, Hulme & Snowling, 1993; Snowling, 1998b). The best known is probably that proposed by Frith (1985) where reading and spelling development is seen as interdependent. A wish to read leads to the initial whole word 'logographic' stage; a wish to write then becomes the pacemaker for the 'alphabetic' stage; and, as reading and spelling become automatic, children move to the third 'orthographic' stage. Seymour and colleagues prefer to consider children's early reading development in terms of foundation processes, principally involving logographic and alphabetic processes and letter-sound knowledge (Duncan, Seymour & Hill, 1997; Seymour & Evans, 1994). This framework encompasses individual variation and preferences, which in turn may be influenced by the teaching and learning methods to which children have been exposed.

The self-teaching hypothesis, presented by Share (1995) and Share and Stanovich (1995), offers an item-based, word-by-word account of learning once children have moved on to the orthographic phase of learning to read. Semantic and contextual information come into play and may help resolve any phonological ambiguities as children, in their own reading, seek to decode new or unfamiliar words. When a consistent phonological code is established for these words, which for normally developing readers may take very few exposures, such words go into the reader's 'bank' of words that can be read apparently effortlessly and automatically. The amount, type and breadth of reading that learners undertake is crucial to their reading development via a process of self teaching. Motivation and interest, therefore, become important as, increasingly, do semantic and syntactic abilities, which are integral to the self-teaching process. Nevertheless, phonological recoding is crucial in self-teaching, and thus the efficiency and integrity of underlying phonological abilities will determine how effectively children are able to learn through independent reading.

As discussed by Snowling (1998b), stage models have their limitations. First, the mechanisms involved in the transition from one stage to the next are not specified. Second, empirical data has challenged the universality of the stages. Reading development is dependent on the teaching methods deployed, and, also, the language in which children are learning to read. Snowling (op. cit.) suggests, therefore, that current research may be best accommodated in a 'connectionist' model that combines semantic and phonological information from the very start of learning. This framework is considered in the sections below.

3.7   MODELS OF READING

The automaticity shown in skilled reading has led to the 'dual route' model where there is a direct 'visual route' to the lexicon (the processor of meaning) or an indirect sub-lexical 'phonological route' to the lexicon. This latter route is considered to be slow and more cumbersome. Dual route models rely quite strongly on dichotomous categorisations or words, i.e. regular/irregular, and high/low frequency, which may better be viewed in terms of continua. It should be noted also that there are a number of assumptions contained in such models, in particular, that phonological processing is confined to sound correspondence at the grapheme (letter) – phoneme (sound) level. Convincing evidence now shows that there are various levels of representation within phonology (Goswami & Bryant, 1990; Treiman & Zukowski, 1991).

The research supporting a dual route model comes primarily from work with adult patients who have various forms of brain injury or insult. These findings may not be applicable to children who are in the process of learning to read and who have not suffered any known neurological damage (Karmiloff-Smith, 1997). Nevertheless, the dual route model continues to influence current theoretical debate (Coltheart & Jackson, 1998).

According to Snowling (1998b), the connectionist framework of 'parallel distributed processing networks' (Plaut, McClelland, Seidenberg & Patterson, 1996) provides the most plausible metaphor in accounting for the cognitive research findings that she reviews. The model is based on computer simulations that use the learning capabilities of artificial neural networks (Plunkett, Karmiloff-Smith, Bates, Elman & Johnson, 1997; Seidenberg & McClelland, 1989). These networks are good at extracting statistical regularities and so come equipped with learning algorithms suited to particular tasks of learning. This means that connectionist models reflect the distribution of the examples they encounter in their training environments.

The simulated model described by Plaut *et al.* (op cit) is trained to read regular words *(mint)*, irregular/exceptional words *(pint)* and non words *(nint)*. The model learns to do so because it develops learning algorithms to take account of both semantic and phonological pathways. In the early stages, the phonological pathway predominates but, as the model 'learns', the semantic pathway becomes increasingly important. The assumption of this model is that fluent readers use a combination of semantic and phonological information during word recognition.

3.8   DYSLEXIA AND THE CONNECTIONIST FRAMEWORK

The connectionist framework has implications for educational practice (Reason, 1998b). If readers need both phonological and semantic information to be able to cope with all types of printed word, continuous text with a rich and varied content plays a central role in reading development. As shared and guided reading of interesting material complements the specific teaching of phonological regularities, in practice, the model encompasses motivational influences (Biggar & Barr, 1996; Pumfrey, 1997) and the importance of culturally relevant contents (Wallace, 1986; Street, 1995, Millard, 1997). Connectionist models, such as that described by Plaut *et al.* (op. cit.), are closely compatible with the process of 'self-teaching' described in Section 3.6.

As outlined by Snowling (1998b), the connectionist model can incorporate different areas and levels of difficulty in terms of continuous variation in underlying skills as they interact with the environment. Within this framework, dyslexia becomes a function of the reciprocal effects of learning opportunities and the type and extent of phonological and semantic strengths and difficulties. It also takes account of orthographic representations as they link with the phonological system (see Section 4.8). These variations can account for individual differences, such as those associated with adequate word reading but poor spelling, where the underlying skills are sufficient for the development of reading but too coarse grained to ensure accurate spelling.

A fully explicit model of skilled reading, allied with a model of how children learn to read, allows us to be neutral about which aspects of learning have been affected. It is thus possible for all or any of the areas of orthography, phonology, syntax or semantics to lead to word reading and spelling difficulties. The converging view, however, of the central role of phonology, in both skilled reading and in accounts of how children become skilled readers, would suggest that weaknesses in phonological processing and representational abilities are highly likely to affect the learner's word reading and spelling development.

It is also possible to fit such models within levels of explanation which are both 'proximal', such as phonological processing, or 'distal', such as neurological functioning (see Section 5.2 for examples in practice). In this sense, causal modelling frameworks, introduced in the next section, accommodate the types and levels of delay/deficit that have been described within the connectionist model in this section.

Models of skilled performance and accounts of how children learn to become skilled readers allow practitioners to put the assessment and intervention required into a useful context. The starting point would be an individual analysis of children's reading and spelling performances and of their learning experiences. Within this context the question of whether a child is dyslexic or not may then be addressed.

3.9   CONCLUSIONS

✦ Consideration of difficulties in learning to read and spell are set in the context of our knowledge of skilled performance and of the way that literacy skills are acquired by young learners.

✦ Word reading involves rapid and automatic mapping of letter strings on to the most likely pronunciation. Skilled spelling also involves an implicit knowledge of the probabilities of particular letter patterns occurring together.

✦ The speech and language abilities and phonological competencies of young pre-reading children can predict their subsequent reading development. The interactions between different facets of early language development are complex and, in terms of predicting later literacy, vary with age and stage of development.

✦ According to current research, phonological coding provides a central unifying thread in the word reading process. However, the role, amount and relative weight of phonological processing, and how complete this has to be, is likely to alter in the course of reading development.

✦ Skilled and fluent readers make little use of contextual clues in word reading other than to clarify the intended meaning when the same spelling has more than one possible meaning. Unlike fluent readers, poor readers require contextual information as a compensatory strategy in assisting word recognition.

✦ The whole language model of reading conceives word reading as a 'psycho-linguistic guessing game'. It is argued that, driven by a search for meaning, the fluent reader makes educated guesses on the basis of the text already read. A crucial assumption is that most words can be 'read' as wholes, visually. The evidence against such an account of reading behaviour is by now incontrovertible. Accurate and fluent word decoding is a pre-requisite for efficient reading for interest and information.

✦ Stage models of the development of word reading and spelling are both of interest in research but also of relevance to educational practitioners. However, the mechanisms involved in the transition from one stage to the next are not specified. Reading development is dependent on the teaching methods employed, and, also, the language in which children are learning to read.

✦ The amount, type and breadth of reading that learners undertake is crucial to their reading development via a process of self teaching. Motivation and interest, therefore, become important, as do semantic and syntactic abilities integral to the self-teaching process. Nevertheless, phonological recoding is crucial in self-teaching, and thus the efficiency and integrity of underlying phonological abilities will determine how effectively children are able to learn through independent reading.

✦ According to a 'connectionist' framework, learners need both phonological and semantic information to be able to read all types of printed word. The framework can incorporate different areas and levels of difficulty in terms of continuous variation in underlying skills as they interact with the environment. Dyslexia can be regarded then as a function of the reciprocal effects of learning opportunities and the type and extent of phonological and semantic strengths and difficulties.

✦ Accounts of skilled performance and of how children become skilled readers allow practitioners to put the assessment and intervention required into a useful context. The starting point is an analysis of children's reading and spelling performances, their learning experiences and their weaknesses in phonological processing and representational abilities. Within this context, the question of whether a child is dyslexic or not may then be addressed.

Section 4: THEORETICAL EXPLANATIONS

4.1 INTRODUCTION

The purpose of this section is to inform readers of theoretical debates concerning the concept of dyslexia through a review and critique of different models. Consequently, the use of the term 'hypothesis' relates here to different theoretical approaches rather than the hypotheses formulated by practitioners in educational psychology assessment and intervention. Sections 5 and 6 of this report will consider implications of theory for practice.

4.2 THE CAUSAL MODELLING FRAMEWORK*

In Section 2.5 we proposed a working definition of dyslexia which stated that *dyslexia is evident when accurate and fluent word reading and/or spelling develops very incompletely or with great difficulty.* We argued that this working definition provided a starting point for testing out theoretical explanations as hypotheses that contributed to our understanding of dyslexia. In Section 3 we considered dyslexia in the context of skilled reading and spelling and the way the skill was acquired by young learners. The research provided the backdrop for the theoretical explanations of learning difficulties considered below.

Much of the debate between different accounts of dyslexia concerns explanations at quite different levels of analysis. We begin this section, therefore, by outlining a framework which can be used in locating different accounts at the appropriate levels of explanation.

The causal modelling framework was developed by Morton and Frith (1995) as a means of portraying known facts about developmental disorders and the hypothesised processes involved. Frith (1995, 1997) has illustrated the way in which this neutral framework can be used to represent and contrast competing theories of dyslexia. In this section the framework is outlined and, in the following sections, it is used to depict the key features of the different theoretical explanations which are described.

The basic framework, which is shown in Figure 4.1, involves three levels of description: the biological, the cognitive and the behavioural. In addition, the framework recognises the operation of environmental factors at all three levels: 'This chain of causal links from brain to mind to behaviour has to be set within the context of environmental and cultural influences' (Frith, 1997, p.2).

✦ THE BIOLOGICAL LEVEL

Observations and facts about the brain are placed at the biological level. Brain functioning can be influenced both by internal genetic factors and external environmental factors, such as quality of nutrition or levels of toxins. As a result of their national inquiry into dyslexia, Pumfrey and Reason (1991) recommended that practitioners ensure that their assessments of dyslexia are undertaken with an awareness of possible neuro-psychological factors and

---

*We would like to thank Professor John Morton of the Institute of Cognitive Neuroscience, University College London, for working with us on the application of the causal modelling framework and for drawing the diagrams to illustrate different theoretical explanations.

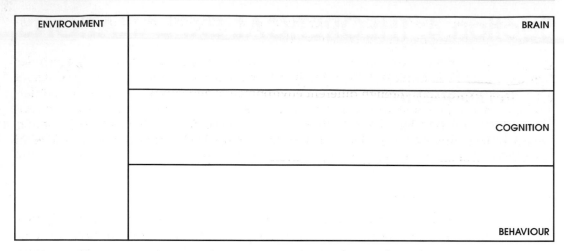

ENVIRONMENT		BRAIN
		COGNITION
		BEHAVIOUR

Figure 4.1: Causal modelling framework (from Morton & Frith, 1995)

are based upon a comprehensive view of literacy development. While educational psychologists are not in a position to carry out any formal neuro-diagnostic procedures or genetic analyses, they may hypothesise about factors within these domains as being central to the development of dyslexia in particular cases. They may also observe signs, such as hereditary patterns, which they suspect may be indicative of hypothesised neurological or genetic factors. They may then refer to a suitably qualified professional for further information or investigation of such possible influences.

Researchers have suggested a number of possible causes: abnormalities in brain asymmetry; abnormal symmetry in the planum temporale; cellular migration; abnormalities in the magnocellular system of the brain; left hemisphere dysfunction; and dysfunction of the language systems around the perisylvian fissure (Hugdahl, 1993; Frith, 1997; Paulesu *et al.*, 1996; Flowers, 1993). Galaburda (1993) suggests that early perceptual anomalies interfere with the establishment of normal cognitive-linguistic structures, coupled with developmental anomalies of cortical structure and brain asymmetry. Nicolson and Fawcett (1995) suggest a cerebellar abnormality as an underlying factor in their automatisation deficit hypothesis. Hynd and Hiemenz (1997) look towards the use of functional magnetic resonance imaging (MRI) procedures over the next decade as a potential tool to investigate the various suggestions for linking cortical anomalies to cognitive processes. Genetic linkage studies with dyslexic families have identified regions on chromosomes 15,1 and, more recently, chromosome 6 (Cardon *et al.*, 1994; Stein & Monaco, 1998).

Empirical neuro-anatomical research, that links brain function to cognitive/linguistic or behavioural concepts, may be useful to educational psychologists, if integrated into explanatory frameworks involving direct measures of cognitive and behavioural functions. Paulesu *et al.* (1996), Galaburda (1993), DeFries *et al.* (1997) and Flynn *et al.* (1992) report examples of such studies, which may be of interest to practitioner psychologists.

Turner (1997) cautions against psychologists offering clinically unsupported, complex neurological explanations of dyslexia in specific cases. Such explanations may risk going beyond what is known and agreed for all individuals. For example, a recent critical review of work on the interhemispheric balance model of dyslexia has brought into question its internal, external and treatment validities (Hynd, 1992; Licht & Spyer, 1994; Van Den Bos,

1996). The evidence base supporting the utility of neurologically-based intervention pro-grammes for dyslexia is yet to be established.

In an overview of the role of brain, mind and behaviour in dyslexia, Frith (1997) concludes that there may be multiple genetic or brain influences. Such factors will result in different phenotypic expressions through different environmental and cultural contexts (e.g. differ-ent languages, different literacy demands in pre-literate and technologically advanced soci-eties). She proposes that the convergence of evidence for a circumscribed, specific, persistent and universal cognitive deficit makes it most likely that the cognitive level of description will offer a unifying theory of dyslexia at the present time.

✦ THE COGNITIVE LEVEL

Hypothesised within-child causes of poor reading performance are situated at the cognitive level. Cognitive skills or deficits/delays must be separated from observed behavioural data because they can only be inferred. The inferred and hypothetical underlying cognitive processes are different in different theories. This is clearly illustrated by the different types of hypotheses that are discussed in this section and modelled using the causal modelling framework. Morton & Frith (1995) include affective factors at this level. While one could argue for effects to be placed at the biological level, as physiological responses, or at the behavioural level, such as facial expressions or voice modulations, the cognitive level is crucial in ascribing meaning to affects and explaining their influence on mental activities and behaviour. Frith (1997) points out that whether a cognitive or affective difficulty will result in literacy problems will not just depend on the nature and severity of the problem but on interactions with environmental factors, such as the complexity of the writing sys-tem involved and the effectiveness of the teaching.

✦ THE BEHAVIOURAL LEVEL

Observations and facts about performance in reading and spelling activities and/or tests are situated at the behavioural level. We can observe directly behaviour, such as words spelt incorrectly or words read inaccurately. Any observations and data collected will be subject to the effects of a range of environmental factors (such as social and physical con-ditions) and within child factors other than those directly related to literacy difficulties (such as motivation) which are themselves open to environmental influences.

4.3   REPRESENTING DIFFERENT THEORETICAL ACCOUNTS OF DYSLEXIA

Some of the theoretical accounts of dyslexia, outlined in the following sections, include comprehensive description at each level in the framework and, in addition, model causal links between the features included at different levels. We need to consider the extent to which available empirical evidence suggests that these should be regarded as alternative accounts of a unitary construct of 'dyslexia', as opposed to being regarded as accounts of different types of dyslexia.

Some of the accounts, outlined below, focus on description at one level of explanation only. While they may be useful in illuminating difficulties experienced by some children and in suggesting possible intervention approaches, there are dangers involved in failing to take a sufficiently comprehensive view. The value of the causal modelling framework, in these cases, is in locating different accounts at the appropriate level(s) of explanation, in identifying conflicts and compatibilities with other accounts, and in delineating the areas within which implications, logically, can be drawn. First we focus on the phonological deficit/delay hypothesis, both because of the broad empirical support that it commands and because of the role phonology is accorded in many other hypotheses in mediating the impact of dyslexia on the acquisition of word reading and spelling skills. These other hypotheses are considered next and the ways in which they differ from the core phonological deficit hypothesis are illustrated. Finally, we describe hypotheses which offer alternative accounts of the difficulties experienced in dyslexia.

4.4 PHONOLOGICAL DELAY/DEFICIT HYPOTHESIS

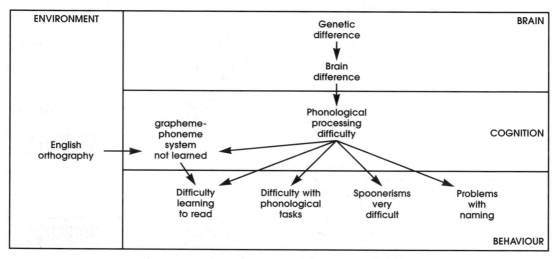

Figure 4.2: Phonological delay/deficit hypothesis

In Figure 4.2 the causal modelling framework is used to represent the hypothesis that dyslexia can be characterised as a core phonological delay or deficit. Phonological processing is broadly defined as the ability to process sounds in spoken language. Phonology is that part of language that concerns the sounds of words, rather than their meanings or grammatical structures. The phonological hypothesis has gained particular prominence in recent years and many of its predictions are supported by a wide range of empirical evidence (Shankweiler & Crain, 1986; Stanovich, 1988; Brady & Shankweiler, 1991; Snowling, 1987, 1991, 1995; Frith, 1997). Indeed, Stanovich (1996) has suggested that the concept of dyslexia can be retained, only logically, if classification as dyslexic is extended to 'all children with problems in phonological coding resulting from segmental language problems' (p.161).

The hypothesis depicted in Figure 4.2 assumes a difference at the brain level. Frith (1997) has suggested that the area affected may be the perisylvian region of the left hemisphere which is known to be involved in phonological processing (Galaburda, 1989; Paulesu *et al.*, 1996). At the cognitive level, it is hypothesised that the neurological difference will cause a weakness in a cognitive component of the phonological system. As Frith (1997) points out, however, such a consequence, although likely, is not inevitable. There may be protective factors or redundancy in the system which allow normal phonological processing to be maintained. If a weakness in phonological processing does result then, in the absence of compensatory factors, it is likely that this will have an impact on aspects of speaking and, through difficulties in the establishment of grapheme-phoneme (letter-sound) links, on the acquisition of literacy skills. This is represented at the behavioural level in the observation of poor reading skills. The phonological weakness, however, is also found to have a number of other effects (see Snowling, 1995, for a review). Some of these, like poor phoneme awareness, will be influenced also by knowledge of grapheme-phoneme correspondences and hence by reading skill. Some other processes, such as poor rapid automatic naming and poor short term auditory memory, are not likely to be directly influenced by reading ability.

4.5   TEMPORAL PROCESSING HYPOTHESIS

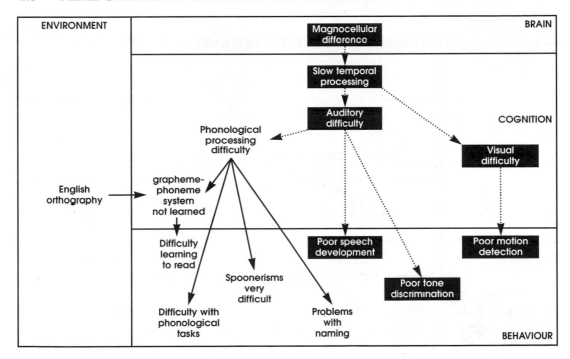

Figure 4.3: Temporal processing hypothesis

Figure 4.3 shows the temporal processing hypothesis advanced by Tallal *et al.* (1997). This involves differences in higher order auditory processing affecting rapid temporal integration of both speech and non-speech stimuli. Individuals described as dyslexic are inclined to have particular difficulty in perceiving intrasyllabic-acoustic differences between speech contrasts involving brief, rapidly changing or transient stimuli, such as perceiving the difference between the syllables /bae/, /dae/ and /gae/. Comparable transient processing difficulties have also been reported in the visual modality (Farmer & Klein, 1995).

At the biological/brain level, differences in the magnocellular layers of the visual and auditory regions of thalamus, identified in the study by Galaburda and Livingstone (1993), have been proposed as potential neuro-biological bases for this difficulty.

Tallal *et al.* also report that the use of computer games, designed to allow children with language difficulties more time to integrate stimuli and progressively improve their temporal integration rates, have resulted in improvements in a number of aspects of language processing, including phonological processing. Further efficacy trials are being undertaken with children who have language difficulties and those who have reading difficulties. Tallal *et al.* argue that the link between speech and language difficulties and reading difficulties results from problems with temporal processing. In order to overcome difficulties with processing information in the tens of milliseconds time range, children with speech and language difficulties typically learn to chunk speech into large units such as words and syllables. Although this eventually facilitates an adequate level of language skills, further difficulties arise when they are asked to discriminate individual phonemes within words in learning to read. Their difficulties in perceiving phonemes are characteristic of the phonological awareness difficulties reported by most investigations of dyslexia.

4.6   SKILL AUTOMATISATION HYPOTHESIS

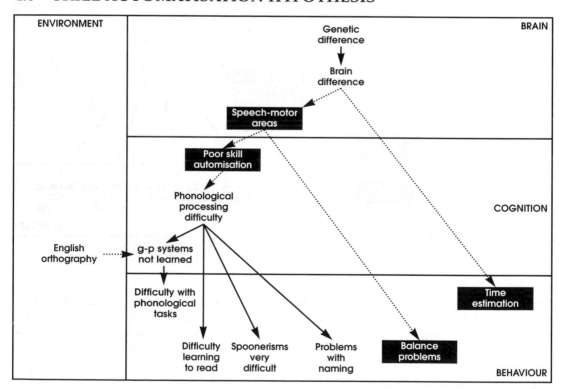

Figure 4.4: Skill automatisation hypothesis

Figure 4.4 represents key aspects of Nicolson and Fawcett's (1995) skill automatisation hypothesis. This hypothesis proposes that dyslexic children have difficulties across a range of skills, including phonological skills, where they are required to perform at a fluent, automatic level and are prevented from employing conscious compensation to overcome their difficulties. For example, they report that dyslexic children have difficulty in balancing without wobbling when prevented from consciously compensating for their difficulties (either by being given a distracting task or by being blindfolded).

At the biological/brain level, Nicolson and Fawcett (1995) hypothesise a cerebellar abnormality which disrupts phonological processing through the effect on language dexterity of a speech motor deficit. They hypothesise that dysfunction in the cerebellum or its neural tracts can account for difficulties in phonological processing, in balance and in estimating time. Nicolson and Fawcett (1995) have developed assessment batteries (DST and DEST) incorporating related test items of phonological processing skills, motor skills and balance (see Appendix C).

4.7   WORKING MEMORY HYPOTHESIS

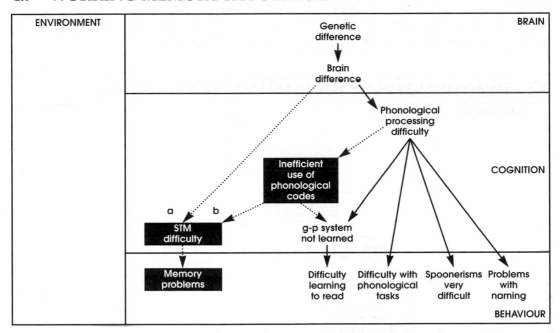

Figure 4.5: Working memory hypothesis

Rack (1994) reports that, *'one of the most reliable and often quoted associated characteristics of developmental dyslexia is an inefficiency in short term memory'* (p.9). This inefficiency, at the cognitive level, appears to be mediated by inefficiencies in the use of phonological codes in short-term memory. It is hypothesised that dyslexic learners make less efficient use of phonological codes and, hence, have more limited short-term memory capacities. Stanovich, Siegel and Gottardo (1997a) report that phonological dyslexics show significantly greater verbal working memory deficits than younger reading-age matched controls and suggest that these deficits may well arise from processing problems at the phonological level. Hulme and Roodenrys (1995) argue that the short-term memory problems of poor readers are not causally related to their poor reading but are an index of other phonological deficits that are a cause of reading difficulties. They also caution against treating 'short term memory' as a unitary concept.

The terms 'short-term memory' (STM) and 'working memory' are sometimes used interchangeably. However, the concept of working memory is more dynamic and focuses on processing and storage demands whereas STM focuses only on storage demands. Working memory is concerned with the interpretation and integration of new information with previously stored information (Baddeley, 1986). Kaufman (1994) links these two aspects of memory to Digits Forwards and Digits Backwards on the WISC, *'Repeating digits in the same order as they are spoken is an automatic task that requires an immediate response with some mediation and does not tax the individual's working memory. Reversing digits, in contrast, requires number manipulation and spatial visualisation to recode the information in working memory'* (p.232).

Mann (1986) argues that memory differences between dyslexic and other readers relate only to information which needs to be linguistically coded, and not to non-verbal information. The desirability of remaining open to other possibilities, in particular individual cases, however, is illustrated by Goulandris and Snowling (1991) who provide evidence, from a single case study on poor memory for visual letter sequences, to suggest visual memory problems as a possible explanation of poor spelling in dyslexia.

4.8 HYPOTHESES THAT INVOLVE VISUAL PROCESSING

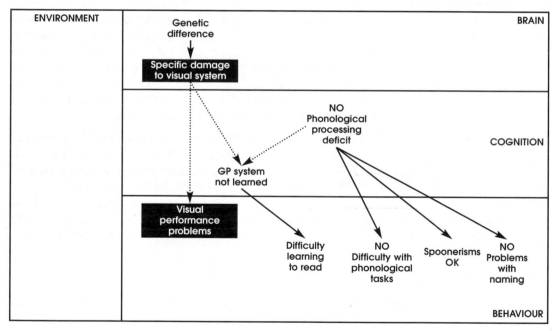

Figure 4.6: Hypotheses that involve visual processing

While current research literature has focused on dyslexia as a language problem, there is continuing interest in many aspects of visual processing (Evans, 1997; Hogben, 1997; Lovegrove, 1994; Willows *et al.*, 1993). It must be stressed, however, that linguistic and visual explanations are by no means mutually exclusive. As concluded by Watson and Willows (1993), 'both scientists and clinicians need to keep an open mind about the possibility that visual processing deficits might contribute in some way to reading disabilities' (p.304).

Visual hypotheses involve optometrics, neurophysiology and cognition. In the area of optometrics, researchers have regarded eye sight as an additional contributory factor rather than the cause of literacy difficulties. A theory of visual discomfort, for example, provides one explanation for the apparent beneficial effects of tinted lenses or overlays for some individuals with reading difficulties, eye strain, headaches or photosensitive epilepsy (Wilkins 1993; Evans & Drasdo, 1991).

It is also argued that children with reading difficulties may have unstable visuo-motor control (Stein, 1994). Originating in the work of Dunlop (1972), Stein and his co-workers conducted a series of studies that pointed to significant differences in binocular fixation stability and in vergence control in dyslexic and normally reading children. A study by Cornelissen *et al.* (1992) has demonstrated that children with unstable fixations are able to reduce the proportion of non-word reading errors if they use only one eye. This is indeed the rationale for giving children monocular occlusion as a treatment option. Stein (1994) admits, however, that this hypothesis is controversial (see Goulandris *et al.*, 1998 and Stein *et al.*, 1998). In response to critique, Stein and his co-researchers have developed more sophisticated measures using infra-red eye movement recordings and computer simulations in investigating the possible contribution of unstable binocular control.

Hogben (1997) provides a clear account of both the terminology and the research concerned with the magnocellular pathway between the retina and the cortex. Over the past ten years, evidence has accumulated that some discrepancy defined dyslexics show deficits in this transient system. Lovegrove (1994) speculates that these findings may reflect individual differences in processing rapidly presented stimuli in all sensory modalities. As there is currently no convincing theory, however, that explains why or how such visual deficits might affect reading, Hogben concludes his review with the comment that, without a coherent theory, the deficit may just be an accidental concomitant of reading difficulties.

It is significant that measures such as visual sequential memory or visual matching seem to play no part in current research literature. Present rationales and methods involve much greater sophistication, including complex technology and accurate timing. In their review of earlier research, Willows *et al.* (1993) conclude that it is unlikely that there are simple visual memory differences between good and poor readers although the possibility of some kind of developmental lag still exists in young children. The validity of test items previously regarded as tapping relevant visual processes is therefore questionable (see Appendix C).

4.9   SYNDROME HYPOTHESIS

Miles (1993) refers to definitions of a syndrome as 'a distinct group of symptoms or signs which, associated together, form a characteristic picture or entity' (*Butterworths's Medical Dictionary*, 1978) or 'signs, symptoms, or other manifestations' especially 'when the cause of the condition is unknown' (*Churchill's Medical Dictionary*, 1989). The term 'syndrome' thus denotes partial knowledge. It also implies that we consider information from diverse fields such as anatomy (Galaburda, 1993; Hynd & Hiemenz, 1997) and genetics (DeFries *et al.*, 1997; Pennington, 1990) as well as different aspects of cognitive research described in other sections of this report.

The work of Tim and Elaine Miles in the 1970s and early 1980s pioneered, in the UK, a particular approach to the assessment of dyslexia as a syndrome, i.e. as a collection of signs and symptoms which can be represented at the behavioural level of the causal modelling framework. Drawing on his clinical work in a university setting, Miles (1983; 1993) noted an identifiable pattern of difficulties that could involve the following: uncertainty over left

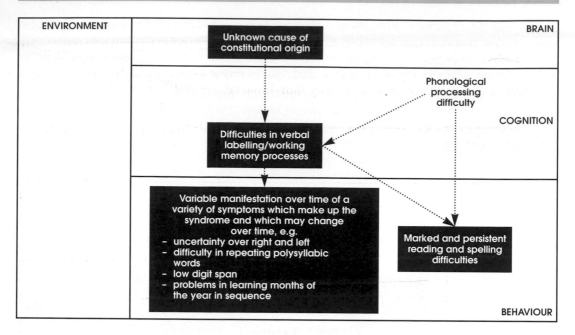

Figure 4.7: Syndrome hypothesis

and right; difficulty in repeating certain polysyllabic words; problems of learning items in series, such as the months of the year; and reduced efficiency in recalling auditorily presented digits.

On initial examination, these items seem to link with several different theoretical rationales at the cognitive level. In discussing their cognitive basis, Miles (1993) comes to the conclusion that each can be explained in terms of verbal labelling/working memory processes and so reflect the core phonological deficit hypothesis considered in Section 4.3 (see also the evaluation of the Bangor Dyslexia Test in Appendix C).

A hypothesis that regards dyslexia as a constellation of difficulties of a constitutional origin, with a basis at the biological level, implies that areas of functioning other than reading and spelling are also affected. Some 'well compensated' learners, for example, may report a range of problems involving disorganisation and slowness while their literacy skills appear to be within 'normal' limits. Conversely, very early language development may be predictive of later literacy difficulties (Lyytinen, 1997; Scarborough, 1990). The developmental dimension of a syndrome hypothesis assumes that underlying problems manifest themselves in different ways throughout the life span of the individual.

In any individual case there may also be substantial variation. For example, there may not be a discernible hereditary pedigree or there may not be difficulties with aspects such as labelling left from right. As recognised by Miles, the primary indicator must be a history of marked and persistent reading and spelling difficulties. Other aspects may be taken as supporting evidence or as pointing to additional special educational needs but are not necessary or sufficient identifiers by themselves. Miles refers to 'clinical judgement' and it is then reasonable to accept that clinical and educational judgement can differ between practitioners.

Arguably, the syndrome hypothesis and the core phonological deficit hypothesis have more in common than has been recognised, although Miles and Miles (1999) argue that phonological deficit theory is not the whole story. Both hypotheses reject exclusionary criteria and look for positive indicators. Both acknowledge that specific literacy problems can occur in children of all levels of cognitive ability. Both can examine associated difficulties, whether cognitive or emotional, in order to specify individual educational needs.

4.10 HYPOTHESES INVOLVING INTELLIGENCE AND COGNITIVE PROFILES

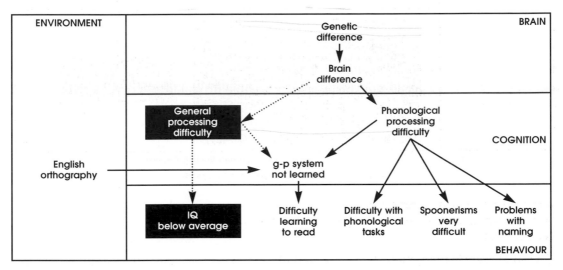

Figure 4.8: Hypotheses involving intelligence and cognitive profiles

The purpose of this section is to consider whether and to what extent reading performance is a function of intelligence rather than to discuss the nature and measurement of intelligence (Gardner, 1984; Howe, 1997; Kaufmann, 1994). It must be taken for granted that a certain level of cognitive ability is necessary for the learning involved and, with large samples, there is indeed a high correlation between reading test results and IQ scores. It is debatable, however, what the required level of IQ should be in the individual case. Research with 'hyperlexic' children (Snowling, 1987) has shown that these children have all the competencies needed for deciphering the text but lack the knowledge and understanding required for comprehending what they read. These children demonstrate the separate, though usually interdependent, dimensions of higher and lower order cognitive skills in reading.

In early reading development, where the emphasis is on phonologically derived information, general ability may have only limited bearing. In the course of reading development, however, semantic and syntactic information becomes particularly important as the cognitive complexity of the text increases (see Section 3.5). Children's knowledge of the world and their other learning clearly impinge on comprehension of what they read. There also may be a positive link between children's general cognitive abilities and their ability to abstract regularities and irregularities from partial information (see Section 3.8). Dyslexic learners' general ability may then also influence their ability to develop compensatory strategies. The relationship between intelligence and reading is thus complex and more likely to be multifaceted and curvilinear rather than a simple linear relationship.

The relevance of the discrepancy approach, based on regression equations on large samples of reading and IQ scores, needs to be considered within this context. As described by Turner (1997), the approach looks for statistically unexpected contrasts between actual educational attainment levels and those predicted on the basis of their IQ scores. A prediction is made from the regression line about what the expected reading level should be on the basis of a given level of intelligence, allowing for chronological age. Siegel (1989, 1992) and Stanovich (1991) argue that the basis for these IQ-achievement discrepancy definitions is an assumption that individuals with low IQ scores should, of necessity, be poor readers. They point out that children with low IQs, who are good readers, have demonstrated that this is not the case (Siegel, 1988, 1992). Although IQ and literacy progress are related (Torgensen, 1986), low IQ is not a sufficient cause of poor reading.

A number of studies have investigated differences between children with IQ-achievement discrepancies and those with poor reading skills but no discrepancy on reading and spelling skills and on cognitive skills related to reading. The research has resulted in a considerable body of evidence, from many countries and with children of different ages, which supports the conclusion that children with reading difficulties of different IQ levels perform similarly on a variety of reading and spelling measures (Friedman & Stephenson, 1988; Siegel, 1988; Seidenberg et. al., 1985; Share et. al.,1987; Felton & Wood, 1992).

According to Stanovich (1998), the notion of the unexpected is irrelevant in the light of current research that can provide explanations, particularly in areas of phonological development. His arguments are pertinent at a time when other researchers, interested in exceptional abilities, have emphasised the multifaceted nature of those abilities and their strong dependence on both environmental and motivational factors (Howe, 1997). The concept of 'potential' and the related concept of 'underachievement' raise questions about the very nature of the measures used and also point to equal opportunities issues in a multicultural and multilinguistic society (Cline & Reason, 1993).

There are two further uses of intelligence tests requiring separate consideration. These are: (1) the use of specific profiles as diagnostic indicators for dyslexia; (2) the use of cognitive assessment data to assist in the formulation of hypotheses about a specific condition, such as dyslexia. Each will be briefly considered in turn.

Frederickson (1999) reviews a range of studies which have evaluated the diagnostic power of certain cognitive assessment profiles, often believed in clinical practice to be typical of dyslexic individuals. Her review focuses in particular on the profile involving the Arithmetic, Coding, Information and Digit Span sub-tests of the Wechsler Intelligence Scale for Children (see Appendix C of this report). Although the ACID profile is found to be statistically more prevalent in samples of dyslexic individuals, the low incidence of the profile (4-5 per cent of a dyslexic sample) means that it is of no real diagnostic utility for individual children. Other cognitive profiles also lack evidence of diagnostic utility. Kaufman (1994), Turner (1997) and Elliot (1998) eschew the notion of any particular cognitive profile as being able to reliably discriminate between dyslexic and non-dyslexic children. Interestingly, Turner (1997) and Spafford (1989) have speculated that a deficit in phonological working memory might be one factor underlying the incidence of an ACID profile.

Cognitive assessment data can, however, aid hypothesis formulation. Assessment instruments such as the Wechsler Intelligence Scale for Children and the British Ability Scales may provide data describing a child's own particular pattern of strengths and weaknesses in cognitive functioning and leading to generation of hypotheses about the role of that pattern in the child's dyslexia. Turner (1997) and Kaufman (1994) both write comprehensively on the subject of using individual cognitive assessment profiles to understand dyslexia/ learning difficulty.

Kaufman (1994) advocates WISC interpretation using an information processing model that explains the processes of input, integration, storage, and output by which the learning difficulty arises. He outlines an approach to 'effortful test interpretation' (p.23) stressing the need for 'detective work' (p.271) by the psychologist in making formulations from information in the area which lies between the child's full scale IQ and the specific subtest scores. For convenience, Kaufman (1994) provides tables summarising the abilities and non-cognitive influences shared by WISC subtests.

Turner (1997) supplements clinical guidelines with dyslexia case studies illustrating the use of both WISC and BAS subtests in the assessment of impaired learning processes. Both authors emphasise the importance of supporting the hypotheses generated from cognitive profile interpretation with data from multiple sources. This needs to include an appraisal of the validity and reliability of test results in the light of children's cultural experiences and life events such as recent trauma.

4.11 SUBTYPE HYPOTHESES

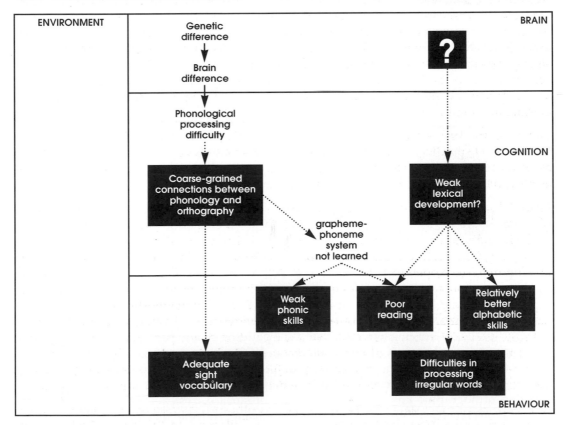

Figure 4.9: A subtype hypothesis drawing on Stanovich *et al.* (1997b)

It is debatable whether psychologists' hypothesising about particular subtypes of dyslexia sensibly constitutes a separate framework of theoretical explanation. The reason for this is that certain of the subtypes identified actually sit within or between other frameworks. Many traditional subtype groupings have broadly tended to stress auditory/visual differences (e.g. Bakker, 1979; Boder, 1973; Thomson, 1989), in line with dual-route reading development theory. The visual/auditory distinction could be accommodated by explanatory frameworks which involve phonological and visual deficit hypotheses. The value of considering subtype explanatory frameworks is that it highlights the possibility that explanatory frameworks may not be mutually exclusive.

Pumfrey and Reason (1991) have questioned the relevance to practitioners of some dyslexia subtyping systems, and Stanovich *et al.* (1997c) argue that much subtyping research has not been grounded in current theories of human information processing or cognitive psychology. Tonnessen (1997) suggests that confusion about the existence or not of dyslexia subgroups has come about because of the lack of an agreed clear definition of the general concept. He reasons that if work in this area had proceeded empirically and inductively, rather than deductively and intuitively, the research community would have had to consider the subgroups before the general group.

Resulting from the considerations above, the following classification systems cannot easily be integrated: Linguistic (L) type/Perceptual (P) type/Mixed linguistic and perceptual type (Bakker, 1979; Masutto *et al.*, 1994); dysphonetic/dyseidetic/mixed (Boder, 1973 – see Appendix C in this report); developmental phonological vs. developmental surface dyslexia (Castles & Coltheart, 1993; Manis *et al.*, 1996); combinations of word attack/word recognition/reading comprehension (Morton, 1994).

Although many critical issues are raised with regard to the internal and external validity of the Bakker (1979) classification system (Licht & Spyer, 1994; Hynd, 1992), the phonological/surface distinction is currently viewed by some as theoretically relevant and well replicated (Coltheart & Jackson, 1998; Stanovich *et al.*, 1997a; Stanovich *et al.*, 1997b; Snowling & Nation, 1997). This distinction postulates two dyslexia subtypes depending upon the severity of the phonological processing impairments. For children exhibiting behavioural characteristics of the phonological subtype, the connections they make between phonology and orthography will be coarse grained. Such children will be able to learn to read words but they will have difficulty in generalising their knowledge to novel word reading. They continue for longer than normal readers to rely on a visual strategy for reading words (Rack *et al.*, 1992). For children in the surface dyslexia subtype, a fully functional reading system may be acquired normally, albeit slowly. The alphabetic skills are mastered but they tend to rely more heavily on a phonological strategy, thus encountering difficulty with pronunciation of irregular words and differentiation of homophones.

This pattern has been taken as evidence for differential impairment in a dual-route model, or as part of the converging evidence that some patterns of developmental dyslexia do not have a phonological basis (Coltheart & Jackson, 1998). Some theorists, however, maintain the phonological deficit hypothesis as central, postulating severe phonological difficulties for the phonological dyslexia and milder phonological difficulties, together with some impaired orthographic knowledge, in the case of surface dyslexia (Snowling & Nation, 1997; Stanovich *et al.*, 1997b). Morris *et al.* (1998), using multiple methods of cluster analysis, identified seven subtypes of reading disability but reported that, 'virtually all children – and subtypes – shared impairments on measures of phonological processing' (p.367).

Other explanations implicate multiple underlying deficits and/or experiential differences, rather than a visual processing problem for surface dyslexic children (Manis *et al.*, 1996; Stanovich *et al.*, 1997a). These arguments lead to the single route connectionist framework (see Sections 3.7 and 3.8) that emphasises individual differences rather than subtypes.

Despite widespread support for the validity of the phonological/surface distinction, there are other considerations. For example, at the cognitive and neuro-psychological levels of analysis, adopted by Nicolson and Fawcett (1995), no evidence of subtypes was found. Furthermore, studies by Ellis *et al.* (1996a, 1996b) found equally substantive individual differences within other groups of matched non-dyslexic children as with dyslexic groups. These comparisons included younger children of the same reading age. In addition, there was no evidence that children in any of the four groups studied, including dyslexic children, clustered into distinct subtypes. It can be concluded, therefore, that it is more appropriate to consider dimensions of individual differences in dyslexia rather than discrete subtypes (Rack *et al.*, 1992).

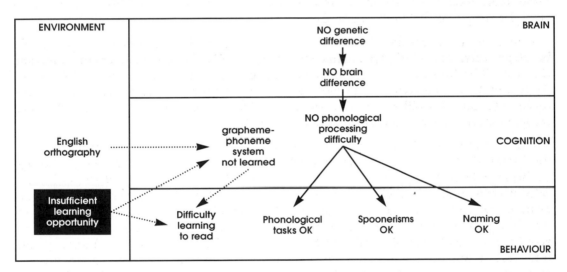

Figure 4.10: Learning opportunities hypothesis

4.12 LEARNING OPPORTUNITIES AND SOCIAL CONTEXT HYPOTHESIS

Learning opportunities and social context hypotheses are based on the assumption that differences in literacy skills performance between children result primarily from differences between them in learning opportunities and experiences, rather than inherent differences (Solity, 1996). Poor learning progress is attributed to children's school- and home-based experiences in learning to read and attention is focused on environmental interventions which alter aspects of the social context, the learning opportunities and the instruction provided. The assumption is that, whatever their individual differences, children will learn given appropriate provision.

It is argued that some of the individual differences that are ascribed causal significance in other theories of dyslexia may simply be indicators of consistent and important differences in different children's social contexts. Solity (1996) suggests that potential sources of learning opportunities (e.g. parental input) might account both for the pre-school differences in phonological awareness and for differences in progress with learning to read. While this appears a less likely explanation for the findings of studies where social context factors, e.g. social class, are taken into account, it is always important to consider the availability of learning opportunities both inside and outside school.

A meta-analysis of 152 studies concluded that 75 per cent of students with specific learning difficulties show social skills deficits that distinguish them from comparison groups (Kavale & Forness, 1996). In addition to considering the possible impact of school failure on student's social and emotional development, researchers have argued that it may be important to investigate family characteristics (Melikian, 1990) and characteristics of the classroom social network (Farmer, Pearl & Van Acker, 1996). The hypothesis, however, has also been put forward that a central nervous system dysfunction, resulting in impaired communication skills, is responsible both for the dyslexic student's literacy difficulties and for their poor social competence (Spafford & Grosser, 1993).

As our definition of dyslexia requires persistent difficulties, notwithstanding appropriate learning opportunities, children whose reading problems are due to inadequate learning opportunities would be expected to make progress when given appropriate help and therefore not be identified as dyslexic. Stanovich *et al.* (1997b), however, have hypothesised that different levels of experience with print may interact with different levels of phonological impairment in producing different patterns of performance. They suggest that relatively low levels of exposure to print combined with relatively mild phonological difficulties may produce a pattern of performance characteristic of 'surface dyslexia' (see Section 4.11). While relatively high levels of exposure to print combined with relatively severe phonological difficulties may produce a pattern of performance characteristic of 'phonological dyslexia'. One advantage of the causal modelling approach is the ease with which such competing accounts of differences in performance can be represented and compared.

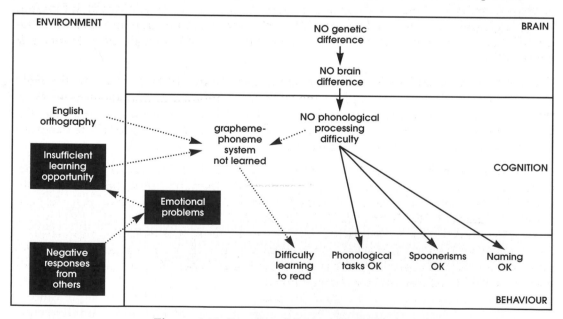

Figure 4.11: Emotional factors hypothesis

4.13 EMOTIONAL FACTORS HYPOTHESIS

It is generally considered that emotional difficulties can be associated with dyslexia (DfEE, 1994, Code of Practice para 3.61). Whilst these affective responses are not the causes, but rather the consequences, of dyslexia, they may contribute to and exacerbate learning difficulties in a complex and incremental way (Pumfrey & Reason, 1991).

Emotional responses do not happen in a vacuum but are closely associated with the environmental, instructional and interpersonal influences outlined in Section 4.12 of this report. Adverse emotional consequences are not inevitable but depend on both individual coping strategies and the way the educational and social context can 'cushion' and support learners experiencing difficulties with basic literacy and associated competencies (Ackerman & Howes, 1986; Adelman, 1989; Biggar & Barr, 1996; Coles, 1989; Hinshaw, 1992; Rourke, 1988; Speece, McKinney & Applebaum, 1985).

Follow-up studies have reported an increasing correlation between reading and behavioural difficulties in the course of primary school education while secondary aged children were more inclined to restlessness and inattentiveness (Jorm et al., 1986; McGee et al., 1988; Pianta & Caldwell, 1990). A Norwegian longitudinal study of 3,000 children demonstrated, through regression analyses, that the best predictors of achievement were of a linguistic-cognitive nature, explaining between 26 per cent and 42 per cent of the variance, while emotional factors explained only 1.2 per cent to 2.7 per cent of the variance (Gjessing & Karlsen, 1989). Negative emotional experiences were reported, however, for a small sub-group of dyslexic children although there were marked individual differences.

Research attempting to clarify the relationship between literacy difficulties and personal and emotional consequences is sparse, not least because of methodological problems (Maughan, 1994). Not only are researchers required to provide operational definitions of learning difficulties, but they also enter debates about definitions and measures of emotional concomitants such as stress (Gentile & McMillan, 1987; Lazarus & Smith, 1988), self-esteem (Casey et al., 1992; Huntington & Bender, 1993; Marsh, 1992; Fairhurst & Pumfrey, 1992), aggression (Cornwall & Bawden, 1992), achievement motivation and causal attribution (Butkowski & Willows, 1980; Dodds, 1994; Pumfrey, 1997; Weiner, 1995; Yasutake & Bryan, 1995).

The effects of stress and anxiety on working memory (Darke, 1988; Zatz & Chassin, 1985) are particularly relevant in the light of the importance afforded to phonological working memory in this report (see Section 4.7 and Gathercole and Baddeley in Appendix C). Despite the paucity of research in this area, Yasutake and Bryan (1995) conclude that positive emotion can enhance children's performance on a variety of tasks.

Several researchers have reported on interviews with dyslexic learners and their parents that elucidate individual experiences and perspectives (Osmond, 1993; Riddick, 1996; Van de Stoel, 1990). There are also case studies (Edwards, 1994) and personal biographies (e.g. Faludy & Faludy, 1996; Hampshire, 1990; Innes, 1991) that describe vividly the concerns and coping strategies of each individual. All these accounts emphasise the importance of the views of the learners themselves. An understanding of the reciprocal effects of instructional circumstances, cognitive processes and the learner's perceptions/emotional experiences is central to educational psychology practice.

4.14 CONCLUSIONS

✦ The purpose of this section is to inform practitioners of research and theory in the area of dyslexia. The term 'hypothesis' is used therefore in relation to different theoretical approaches, developed by academic researchers, to explain the concept of dyslexia. Implications with regard to hypotheses formulated in educational psychology assessment and intervention are considered separately in Sections 5 and 6.

✦ The working definition introduced in Section 2.5 provides a starting point for the present review of different theoretical approaches and their associated research bases. Each approach is considered within a causal modelling framework involving three levels of analysis: the biological (brain), the cognitive and the behavioural.

✦ Some of the theoretical accounts of dyslexia include comprehensive description at each level in the framework and, in addition, model causal links between the features included at different levels. It is important to consider the extent to which available empirical evidence suggests that these should be regarded as alternative accounts of a unitary construct of 'dyslexia', as opposed to being regarded as accounts of different types of dyslexia.

✦ The phonological deficit/delay hypothesis provides the main focus, both because of the broad empirical support that it commands and because of the role phonology is accorded in many of the other hypotheses in mediating the impact of dyslexia on the acquisition of word reading and spelling skills. The following hypotheses include phonological processing as a major component:

 – the temporal order hypothesis that focuses on the speed of processing required in integrating speech and non-speech stimuli;

 – the skill automatisation hypothesis which proposes that underlying brain mechanisms affect a range of tasks requiring rapid and automatic processing;

 – the working memory hypothesis which postulates particular difficulties in processing and storing information that is linguistically coded.

✦ The syndrome hypothesis and the core phonological deficit/delay hypothesis have more in common than may have been recognised. Both hypotheses reject exclusionary criteria and look for positive indicators, including phonological processing and memory. Both acknowledge that particular literacy problems can occur in children of all levels of cognitive ability. Both can examine associated difficulties, whether cognitive or emotional, in order to specify individual educational needs.

✦ While current research has focused on dyslexia as a language problem, there is continuing interest in many aspects of visual processing. Measures, however, such as visual sequential memory or visual matching, previously regarded as tapping relevant visual processes, seem to play no part in current research literature. Present methods involve much greater sophistication, including complex technology and accurate timing.

✦ The validity of identifying dyslexia, in terms of statistically unexpected contrasts between actual literacy attainments and those predicted on the grounds of IQ scores, can be questioned on many grounds. These include the body of evidence showing that children of different IQ levels perform similarly on a variety of measures of reading and spelling.

+ Profiles of test scores obtained from batteries designed to assess overall cognitive performance (e.g. the BAS and the WISC) can aid understanding of the learners particular strengths and weaknesses. However, no particular cognitive profile can discriminate between children with or without literacy difficulties of a dyslexic nature. Furthermore, it is important to consider the validity and reliability of test results in relation to children's cultural experiences and life events, such as recent trauma.

+ Research on subtypes of dyslexia is inconclusive. Much of the work has not been grounded in current theories of cognitive processing. In cognitive research, the debate contrasts dual-route models (involving visual and phonological pathways to the semantic system) with interactive/connectionist models in which the degree of phonological difficulty accounts for different types/levels of word reading and spelling difficulty. There is agreement, however, that dimensions of individual differences in dyslexia are more important than discrete subtypes.

+ Learning opportunities and social context hypotheses are based on the assumption that differences in literacy skills performance between children result primarily from differences between them in learning opportunities and experiences, rather than inherent differences. It seems more appropriate, however, to consider the interaction between learning experiences and individual differences in producing different patterns of performance.

+ Emotional difficulties can be associated with dyslexia. Whilst these affective responses are not the causes, but rather the consequences, of dyslexia, they may contribute to, and exacerbate, learning difficulties in a complex and incremental way. Consequently, an understanding of the reciprocal effects of instructional circumstances, cognitive processes and the learner's perceptions/emotional experiences is central to educational psychology practice.

Section 5: IMPLICATIONS FOR EDUCATIONAL PSYCHOLOGY ASSESSMENT AND INTERVENTION

5.1 A FRAMEWORK FOR PSYCHOLOGICAL ASSESSMENT AND INTERVENTION

The present report builds on publications that provide guidance for educational psychology assessment and intervention in general (see Appendix D, DECP, 1999) and statutory assessments in particular (AEP, 1998). These documents emphasise the multi-faceted nature of educational psychology assessment. Not only are individual and instructional variables taken into account, but also social, motivational and organisational ones too. The role of practitioners is then to investigate a range of possible explanations, and their interactions, in order to test out hypotheses that can lead to workable plans of action.

The DECP framework for psychological assessment and intervention is reproduced in Appendix D. A diagram in the report describes the work of educational psychologists as a cycle of clarification, consultation, observation, investigation, hypothesis generation, intervention, evaluation and further clarification. While the present report focuses primarily on the assessment of word reading and spelling, comprehensive assessment involves the evaluation of strengths, weaknesses and contributory factors in other relevant areas of learning.

5.2 FROM THEORETICAL BASIS TO EDUCATIONAL ASSESSMENT

In Section 2.5 we have argued that, in scientific enquiry, a working definition of dyslexia should be separated from any theoretical or causal explanations which can then be treated as hypotheses to be investigated and evaluated. Sections 3 and 4 of this report have outlined different areas of research and theory relevant to the working definition.

Section 3 has summarised research on skilled performance and the way children learn to read and write. Based on this knowledge, assessment can start with an analysis of reading and spelling and the instructional experiences of the learner. It can examine particular patterns of strengths and weaknesses that emanate from the interaction between the skills children bring to the task of learning to read and the environments to which they are exposed.

Section 4 has considered different theoretical explanations of dyslexia in the light of what we now know about literacy development as outlined in Section 3. These theoretical explanations have been expressed in the form of a series of hypotheses where each presents a particular kind of analysis that can contribute to our understanding of the individual case. While the explanations are not mutually exclusive, they stress different aspects as illustrated in the causal modelling framework introduced in Section 4. Some hypotheses are supported by a body of convincing research while others fare less well in the evaluations provided in that section.

It is useful to distinguish between 'proximal' and 'distal' causes of dyslexia (Coltheart & Jackson, 1998), where the 'proximal' refers to observations of processes involved in word reading and spelling (e.g. poor phonic knowledge) and the 'distal' to constitutional or environmental causes. The role of educational psychology is to appraise each area and to consider their reciprocal effects on learning. For example, constitutional determinants may be alleviated or exacerbated by environmental and educational influences. As the aim is to link assessment with intervention, distal causes involving neuro-anatomy and genetic factors do not by themselves directly inform educational practice. A hereditary pattern, for example, does not identify the nature and extent of dyslexic difficulties although its presence can provide corroborative evidence.

The syndrome hypothesis is based on a 'distal' biological explanation that leads to cognitive mechanisms involving phonological processing and phonological working memory. According to the syndrome hypothesis, however, these processes can affect other associated areas of learning such as aspects of mathematics or organisational skills. While comprehensive assessment does consider all relevant areas of learning, in our view dyslexia cannot be identified through an examination of associated difficulties alone. The working definition adopted by this report requires evidence that accurate and fluent word reading and/or spelling has been achieved very incompletely or with great difficulty.

At the cognitive level, hypotheses involving phonological, orthographic or working memory processes are 'proximal' when their effects can be observed at the behavioural level. However, within the theoretical framework adopted in this report (see Sections 3.7 and 3.8), dyslexia becomes a function of the reciprocal effects of learning opportunities and the type/extent of phonological and semantic strengths and difficulties. As shown in the extensive research undertaken by Vellutino *et al.* (1996), cognitive information is most meaningful in the light of monitored intervention. Consequently, it is important to examine the teaching that has taken place in order to interpret assessments relating to underlying reading processes.

5.3   ASSESSMENT IN PRACTICE

In considering implications for practice, we need to start with the working definition of dyslexia reproduced in Table 5.1. This definition logically requires that three aspects be evaluated through the assessment process:

1. that the pupil is learning/has learnt accurate and fluent word reading and/or spelling very incompletely;

2. that appropriate learning opportunities have been provided;

3. that progress has been made only as a result of much additional effort/instruction and that difficulties have, nevertheless, persisted.

TABLE 5.1: A WORKING DEFINITION OF DYSLEXIA

Dyslexia is evident when accurate and fluent word reading and/or spelling develops very incompletely or with great difficulty. This focuses on literacy learning at the 'word level'í and implies that the problem is severe and persistent despite appropriate learning opportunities. It provides the basis for a staged process of assessment through teaching.

The steps that can be taken, by educational psychologists, teachers, parents and the learners themselves to collect assessment information, in relation to each of these essential components of the definition, are considered in the sections that follow. It is assumed that, with increased knowledge of literacy learning and literacy difficulties in the primary school, monitored intervention can take place early enough to ensure that the process of interactive assessment and teaching does not result in any unnecessary delay for those learners with severe and persistent difficulties. Nevertheless, there may be instances where personal and educational circumstances are such that the persistence of difficulties will need to be ascertained in more indirect ways.

5.4 ASSESSING AND EVALUATING ACCURACY AND FLUENCY OF WORD READING AND SPELLING

In judging whether reading and spelling acquisition is 'very incomplete', the psychologist will make comparisons between the levels achieved by the pupils and those required/expected of them. These requirements/expectations may be established in a number of ways:

✦ They may be expressed normatively, in relation to typical performance of other pupils of the same age. A number of standardised tests are available to educational psychologists and teachers that enable such comparisons to be made. Cook (1999) reviews 12 such reading and spelling tests and also provides evidence of their limitations.

✦ They may also be expressed in terms of performance criteria that define realistic accuracy/fluency levels for particular tasks. Educational psychologists may be involved in advising schools on the construction of informal reading inventories (Rubin, 1997) from a series of literacy related tasks or graded passages that reflect the teaching that has taken place. This can be an effective means for monitoring the progress of all pupils and 'noticing' at an early stage any pupils whose learning programme needs to be adjusted.

✦ Observations of the child's learning behaviour in relation to reading and writing tasks provide important clues regarding individual strategies and errors that reflect a very different pattern of performance than would be expected from children of that age.

To conclude that acquisition of reading and spelling skills is 'very incomplete' will depend on the age and developmental stage of the learner. For the educational psychologist such a conclusion will trigger an investigation of hypothesised factors that may be important in understanding the nature of the difficulties being experienced and in identifying ways of alleviating or overcoming them.

Appendix C evaluates a selection of commercially available tests designed to measure cognitive processes associated with dyslexia. As shown in the theoretical rationales described for each test, the measures reflect different hypotheses outlined in Section 4 of this report. The evaluations show that some of the tests are better supported by current research than others and that information about their standardisation is also very variable. The evaluations demonstrate that no one test can be considered obligatory in educational psychology assessments.

Several tests have been developed for the purposes of tapping phonological competencies. It is important to bear in mind, however, that continuing research may show that current measures are not necessarily reflecting all relevant aspects. Furthermore, performance on tests involving phoneme awareness is influenced by knowledge of grapheme-phoneme correspondences and the reading skills developed by the learner. Hence test results need to be interpreted in the light of the learners' experiences of literacy and the instruction received. Nevertheless, when linked with curriculum-related assessment, these measures, together with observations of reading and spelling competencies and strategies, provide applicable information for ascertaining the severity of phonological difficulties and for the planning of intervention.

The observation of visual processes is complicated by the fact that simple memory of visual patterns, as introduced in earlier tests, is no longer relevant (see Section 4.8 and Appendix C). Research techniques that suggest a possible link between parafoveal, phonological and temporal processing are currently too complex to be translated into educational practice. At the optometric (biological) level, however, checks can be made with regard to visual acuity and discomfort (see Section 4.8) although these aspects are not direct causes of dyslexia.

Educational psychology assessments may refer to test scores from batteries of tests such as BAS and WISC designed to tap aspects of cognitive performance. As shown in the reviews in Section 4.10 and Appendix C, these tests can be informative when pointing to strengths and weaknesses in the individual case. However, no particular pattern of sub-test scores can be regarded as necessary or sufficient in deciding whether and to what extent learning difficulties can be described as dyslexic.

5.5   ASSESSING LEARNING OPPORTUNITIES IN THE CLASSROOM

The second requirement arising from the working definition is to establish that appropriate learning opportunities have been provided, and/or to provide them and monitor progress. Practitioners can start by drawing on the range of research evidence on the characteristics of effective instruction generally. Readers are referred to Yesseldyke and Christenson (1987) and Frederickson and Monsen (1999) for summaries of aspects of this research, together with information about related assessment tools available to educational psychologists.

Yesseldyke and Christenson (1987) describe The Instructional Environment Survey (TIES) which uses classroom observation and pupil and teacher interview to assess the instructional environment as it relates to an individual pupil. That emphasis, on the inter-relationship between the learning environment and the individual pupil, is important because pupils within the same classroom differ in how they perceive and experience the same events (Ames & Archer, 1988). TIES collects information on 12 aspects of effective instruction listed below.

Instructional presentation: Instruction is presented in a clear and effective manner; directions contain sufficient information for the student to understand what kinds of behaviors or skills are to be demonstrated; and the student's understanding is checked before independent practice

Classroom environment: The classroom is controlled efficiently and effectively; there is a positive, supportive classroom atmosphere; time is used productively.

Teacher expectations: There are realistic yet high expectations for both the amount and accuracy of work to be completed, and these are communicated clearly to the student.

Cognitive emphasis: Thinking skills needed to complete assignments are communicated explicitly to the student.

Motivational strategies: The teacher has and uses effective strategies for heightening student interest and effort.

Relevant practice: Student is given adequate opportunity to practice with appropriate materials.

Academic engaged time: The student is actively engaged in responding to academic content; the teacher monitors the extent to which the student is actively engaged and redirects the student when the student is not engaged.

Informed feedback: The student receives relatively immediate and specific information on his or her performance or behaviour; when the student makes mistakes, correction is provided.

Adaptive instruction: The curriculum is modified to accommodate the student's specific instructional needs.

Progress evaluation: There is direct, frequent measurement of the student's progress toward completion of instructional objectives; data on pupil performance and progress are used to plan future instruction.

Instructional planning: The student's needs have been assessed accurately and instruction is matched appropriately to the results of the instructional diagnosis.

Student understanding: The student demonstrates an accurate understanding of what is to be done in the classroom.' (Yesseldyke & Christenson, 1987, p.22).

5.6 ASSESSING LEARNING OPPORTUNITIES WITHIN THE NATIONAL LITERACY STRATEGY

Beard (1999) reviews the research basis and educational precedents of the National Literacy Strategy (NLS) (DfEE, 1998) and shows that the NLS draws extensively on work relating to school and teacher effectiveness and on research in the area of literacy acquisition.

Within the context of the NLS, dyslexia can be defined as marked and persistent problems at the word level of the NLS framework. This enables practitioners to evaluate learning opportunities and teaching methods within a mainstream educational setting. There are two interdependent questions. First, to what extent is the NLS curriculum appropriate for struggling literacy learners whether they are regarded as dyslexic or not? Second, in what ways are the instructional approaches introduced under the heading of dyslexia similar or different to those in general use with all children? Pietrowski and Reason (in press) address these questions. They outline word level learning within the NLS and then consider the teaching approaches in relation to those commonly recommended under the heading of dyslexia.

Overall, the NLS framework can provide a pathway for the cumulative, hierarchical and incremental presentation of word level targets. The Reception Year places emphasis on the securing of a confident knowledge of phoneme/grapheme correspondences in line with research regarding the importance of knowledge and experience at school entry of rhyme, alliteration and letter. The Reception Year targets appear both informed and acceptable. However, the Year 1 Term 3 and Year 2 Term 1 targets currently require a pace and momentum that will present many teachers, children and their parents with considerable demands. The lack of time may compromise the development of word level knowledge and skills of some of the children. It is, for example, possible that summer term birth children, still five years old as they complete Term 3, will be considered to have special needs or dyslexic difficulties simply because the pace is too fast and the coverage too superficial. In the light of experience, therefore, aspects of the NLS are likely to be re-examined.

Established learning theory has stressed the importance of repetitive and cumulative practice to the point of 'mastery' (Kulik, 1991; Lindsley, 1992). Evidence also demonstrates the effectiveness of teaching approaches that introduce code instruction in the context of reading and writing meaningful text (Adams, 1993; Hatcher, Hulme & Ellis, 1994; Wasik & Slavin, 1994). Furthermore, motivation is developed through ensuring that the learner has a sense of competence and control when undertaking the learning (Ames & Archer, 1988). Drawing on these considerations, Pietrowski and Reason (in press) compare three kinds of commercially published materials with a strong emphasis on the teaching of phonics. First, those developed for all children as meeting the requirements of the NLS at the word level; second, those intended for learners making slower progress in literacy; and, third, those targeted at learners regarded as having difficulties of a dyslexic nature. The materials are audited in terms of eight questions:

1. *A comprehensive model:* With their focus on phonics, do the materials reflect a comprehensive model of reading and/or spelling development, i.e. NLS searchlights that include comprehension of the text as a whole and the anticipation of words and letter sequences?

2. *Progression:* Do the materials show a clear progression of phonological targets, starting from phonological awareness and moving gradually to more advanced phonic structures?

3. *Speaking and listening:* Are children exploring and reinforcing the learning of phonological regularities through both speaking and listening?

4. *Reading and writing:* Are children exploring and reinforcing the learning of phonological regularities through both reading and writing?

5. *Assessing to teach:* Do the materials provide guidance on 'assessing to teach', i.e. on assessing what the children know in order to plan, in appropriately small steps, what should be learnt next?

6. *Mastery learning:* Are the materials based on 'mastery learning', i.e. on planned repetition and revision that ensures the retention of what has been learnt?

7. *Role of the learner:* In terms of motivational influences, is there explicit guidance on the involvement of the children themselves in setting own targets and monitoring progress?

8. *Home-school links:* Is there clear guidance on how parents and carers can help their children at home?

The comparisons show that materials developed for all children are more likely to have a comprehensive model of literacy as their major emphasis. Most of the special programmes, in contrast, may contain an implicit assumption that the learning of phonics is but one element of literacy but explicit links between text, sentence and word levels are not made. The headings 'assessing to teach' and 'mastery learning' bring out the differences between the publications. It seems that those materials intended for learners making slower progress place an even greater emphasis on 'assessing to teach' than do the programmes developed under the heading of dyslexia. Both kinds of special programmes have as their major emphasis 'mastery learning', which remains implicit but not explained in the general programmes.

The eight questions highlight the similarities and differences between the approaches included in the comparison. Of particular note is the issue of reciprocal assessment and teaching, i.e. 'assessing to teach'. If those following the materials developed under the heading of 'dyslexia' assume that the learner inevitably needs to start from the beginning of the programme and plough through every aspect of it, then this may result in frustration and boredom. Conversely, the general programmes, and the NLS itself, do not seem to provide enough guidance or detail on how to establish what each child has learnt and how to plan and teach following the principles of 'mastery learning'. If these aspects were addressed more explicitly, the teaching materials would be suitable for all children, including those with learning difficulties of a dyslexic nature, and would provide the basis for the kind of inclusive practices in schools advocated by Ainscow (1998).

5.7   ASSESSING PERSISTENCE

The third requirement of the working definition is to ascertain that progress has been made only as a result of considerable additional effort/instruction and that difficulties have, nevertheless, persisted. In order to meet this requirement educational psychologists work in collaboration with other professionals and draw on the information provided by teachers, parents and the learners themselves in relation to developmental and educational history.

In evaluating response to additional teaching, educational psychologists have available means of monitoring rate of learning progress through Single-subject Experimental Research (Neuman & McCormick, 1995; Richards *et al.*, 1999) and Precision Teaching (Lindsley, 1992; Solity & Bull, 1987). These methods offer a set of strategies for carrying out focused assessments over time of pupil performance and for recording progress in a way that facilitates judgements about educational needs and provides information on what works for particular pupils.

It is important to stress, however, that these methods are not, as such, approaches to instruction but to monitoring and evaluation. The teaching content needs to be informed by an understanding of the processes that facilitate learning in general (Section 5.5 above) and literacy learning in particular (see Section 3). For example, the importance of metacognitive strategies has now gained prominence (Brenna, 1995; Brown, 1996; Fisher, 1998). As precision teaching focuses on fluency as well as accuracy, it provides a useful means for monitoring. In practice, it involves the following five steps:

1. Specify the desired pupil performance in observable, measurable terms.

2. Sample and record performance.

3. Chart progress on a daily basis.

4. Analyse the progress charts to see whether progress is satisfactory or whether changes are needed in order to accelerate progress.

5. Reconsider the teaching approaches being used with the pupil.

The extent to which Precision Teaching is currently used in the UK is unclear. In the 1980s many articles were published describing applications of the approach (Booth & Jay, 1981,

Booth & Jewell, 1983; Faupel, 1986; Raybould & Solity, 1982, Williams & Muncey, 1982). According to Kessissoglou & Farrell (1995) active interest has continued in American journals but there is little recent British research literature.

There is current evidence also to show that when teachers follow the approach they recognise its value (Hasbrouck, Woldbeck, Ihnot & Parker, 1999). As accountable and evidence-based school management has become more developed over the past 15-20 years, it may be expected that monitoring, on the basis of methodology such as Precision Teaching, would now be more congruent with general teaching practices. With regard to the assessment of dyslexia, such methodology offers:

✦ opportunities to fine tune the learning offered to pupils within the context of general programmes such as the National Literacy Strategy,

✦ opportunities to monitor pupil performance and to establish the extent to which difficulties persist across interventions and over time.

The approaches to assessment described in this section can also generate the data needed by LEAs to ensure that additional resources are accessed in a fair and accountable manner (see Section 6). Through the use of progress charts (Faupel, 1986), trends can become apparent over relatively short time periods and make it possible to assess persistence without introducing delay into the process of assessment. The pupil will in any case be receiving daily input and monitoring during this period.

5.8   A NETWORK OF RECIPROCAL EFFECTS

The previous sections have shown how assessment of cognitive processes interacts with evaluations of the learning opportunities and teaching methods available to the child. With the current emphasis on evidence-based practice, it would be ideal if educational psychologists and teachers had access to comprehensive literature surveys that reviewed and summarised relevant evidence on the effectiveness of commonly used approaches. Unfortunately, such an accessible database is currently lacking. Connor (1994) points to the 'considerable discrepancy between work relating to the aetiology and form of dyslexia, and evidence concerning interventions' (p.114). Nevertheless, the information outlined in the present report can lead to the consideration of a network of reciprocal effects through the following sequence of observations:

– At the behavioural level observations start from a determination of the severity and persistence of problems with word reading and spelling. Reasons are then explored in areas involving phonological and orthographic awareness and memory and take account of compensatory styles, such as heavy reliance on context when reading, and unhelpful coping strategies, such as the avoidance of frustrating learning opportunities.

– Observed behaviours reflecting hypothesised cognitive mechanisms are mediated by an appraisal of learning opportunities and teaching methods. Learners may perform relatively well in assessments because of the teaching that has taken place. Conversely, poor performance may not only reflect cognitive mechanisms but also mirror insufficient learning opportunities.

– Learning opportunities and teaching methods are, in turn, considered in the light of the knowledge we have about those aspects that generally enhance learning, reading/spelling acquisition and the cognitive mechanisms that assist or impede that learning.

- An evaluation of the role that social and emotional responses play in contributing to the literacy difficulties also takes account of environmental, instructional and interpersonal influences. Adverse emotional consequences are not inevitable, however, but depend on individual coping strategies and the way the educational and social context can support learners experiencing difficulties.

5.9 CONCLUSIONS

✦ While focusing primarily on word reading and spelling, the present report is located within a wider framework for psychological assessment and intervention that involves all relevant areas of experience and learning.

✦ The working definition of dyslexia adopted in this report requires that three aspects be evaluated through the assessment process:

- That the pupil is learning/has learnt accurate and fluent word reading and/or spelling very incompletely;

- that appropriate learning opportunities have been provided;

- that progress has been made only as a result of much additional effort/instruction and that difficulties have, nevertheless, persisted.

✦ With increased knowledge and awareness of literacy learning and literacy difficulties in the primary school, it is assumed that monitored intervention can take place early enough to ensure that the process of interactive assessment and teaching does not result in any unnecessary delay for those learners with severe and persistent difficulties. Nevertheless, there may be instances where personal and educational circumstances are such that the persistence of difficulties will need to be ascertained in more indirect ways.

✦ The accuracy and fluency of word reading and spelling can be assessed normatively through standardised tests and informally through a series of literacy related tasks that reflect the teaching that has taken place.

✦ The conclusion that the acquisition of reading and spelling is 'very incomplete' depends on the age and developmental stage of the learner. It triggers an investigation of factors that may be important in understanding the nature of the difficulties being experienced and in identifying ways of overcoming or alleviating them.

✦ Appendix C evaluates a selection of commercially available tests designed to measure cognitive processes associated with dyslexia. The evaluations demonstrate that no one test can be considered obligatory in educational psychology assessments.

✦ Several tests have been developed for the purposes of tapping phonological competencies and are useful when interpreted in the light of the learners' experiences of literacy and the instruction received.

✦ The assessment of visual processes is complicated by the fact that simple memory of visual patterns, as introduced in earlier tests, is no longer relevant.

◆ Assessments referring to cognitive test scores within batteries of tests such as the BAS and WISC can be informative when pointing to strengths and weaknesses in the individual case. However, no particular pattern of test scores can be regarded as necessary or sufficient in deciding whether and to what extent learning difficulties can be described as dyslexic.

◆ In assessing overall learning opportunities, psychologists can draw on a range of research that describes the characteristics of effective instruction.

◆ In the context of the National Literacy Strategy, dyslexia can be defined as marked and persistent problems at the word level of the framework. With explicit guidance on 'assessing to teach' and the principles and practices of 'mastery learning' the framework provides a good basis for developing inclusive practices.

◆ The evaluation of persistence in the light of response to additional teaching can involve the monitoring of rate of learning progress through methods such as single-subject experimental research and precision teaching. These methods offer a set of strategies for carrying out focused assessments of pupil performance over time and for recording progress in a way that facilitates judgements about accuracy and fluency of performance.

◆ The information considered in this section can be conceptualised as a network of reciprocal effects involving literacy performance, hypotheses about underlying processes and appraisal of learning opportunities and teaching methods.

Section 6: SPECIAL EDUCATIONAL NEEDS AND DYSLEXIA

6.1 THE CONCEPT OF SPECIAL EDUCATIONAL NEEDS

Recent and regularly revised legislation aims to address the special educational needs of school-aged children experiencing learning difficulty of one kind or another and to improve their opportunities to participate in the school curriculum (DfE, 1981; DfE, 1989; DfEE, 1994; DfEE, 1996; DfEE, 1997). The procedural framework and philosophy of this wing of social policy has been subject to much public, professional and academic debate (Barton, 1988; Ainscow, 1991; Solity, 1991; The Audit Commission, 1992; Wolfendale, 1993; Booth, 1994; Dyson, 1994; Armstrong, 1995; DfEE, 1997). At present, there is national guidance on those conditions which may give rise to special educational needs and the recommendation that procedures for identification at a local level are made as consistent and transparent as possible (DfEE, 1994, 3.48). At a national level, special educational needs are circularly defined in relation to special educational provision:

A child has 'special educational needs' for the purposes of this Act if he has a learning difficulty which calls for special educational provision to be made for him. (Para 312, Education Act 1996)

There is stated to be a continuum of special educational needs and of provision, represented by the incremental stages in the Code of Practice on the Identification and Assessment of Special Educational Needs (forthwith referred to as 'The Code of Practice') (DfEE, 1994, 1.2). Several points are important for interpretation:

✦ The definition allows for variation in the manifestation of special educational needs since what provision is considered to be special may vary between teachers, schools and Local Education Authorities.

✦ The picture is further complicated by the fact that a child can receive special provision from both a school and a Local Education Authority simultaneously. The Code of Practice (1994) proposes that for children with the most complex special educational needs, the special provision to be made by school is distinguished from that to be made by the Local Education Authority (DfEE, 1994 4.28).

✦ Special educational needs are individually described (DfEE, 1994, 3.47) and so simple equivalences between children in obvious aspects of provision, such as hours of specialist teaching support or involvement of the special educational needs co-ordinator, can not be assumed.

✦ Some aspects of special educational needs, such as motivational and emotional consequences, are difficult to quantify and incorporate to the notion of the overall learning difficulty.

✦ Some aspects of provision, such as curriculum differentiation or positive reinforcement, are likewise not easy to define operationally in all cases (DfEE, 1997, 1.2).

✦ The idea of a continuum of provision may be inaccurate and more realistically described as differing patterns of provision (Booth, 1994).

✦ In reality, the learning difficulty and the special educational needs are one and the same thing. Special educational needs are a post hoc, child-centred construction of the learning difficulty following from the agreement to respond to the learning difficulty with provision that is considered to be special.

Taken together, implications are that a child at a particular stage of the special educational needs register in one class/school would not necessarily require or expect to receive the same kind, pattern and amount of provision as another similar child, even in the same class (DfEE, 1997, 1.2). National special educational needs criteria which unambiguously describe each disability condition at each level of severity might give a consistent picture of special educational needs and the responsibility for provision, but this is generally thought to be unworkable (DfEE, 1997, 3.18).

The resultant fluidity in constructions of special educational needs across localities (classrooms, schools and LEAs) leads some theorists to question the validity and utility of the concept. They prefer instead to focus upon the effects of curriculum and school organisation in accommodating the whole variety of students' individual educational needs (Ainscow, 1991; Wang, 1991; Thousand & Villa, 1991; Booth 1994).

Thus, it is not presently possible to make universal, operational descriptions about each stage of special educational needs for each category of disability. (DfEE, 1997, 1.1) Cut-off points to indicate severity of need are essentially arbitrary, relating most closely to local education authority policy about administration of provision. Indeed, it has been argued that the stages on the special educational needs register relate more to administration of provision than they do to either the actual provision made or the nature of the child's difficulties (Booth, 1994).

The guidance on special educational needs serves as a flexible framework supporting parents, schools and LEAs in planning how to address the educational needs of individual children who are vulnerable or challenging. The direction of this joint work will depend upon agreements reached about formulation (nature of the learning difficulty), provision (how it is to be addressed) and administration (who will ensure that it is addressed). These in turn depend in part upon local authority policy.

6.2   SPECIAL EDUCATIONAL NEEDS AND DYSLEXIA

Legislation allows for the formal identification of dyslexia as one kind of learning difficulty that may give rise to special educational needs, but which in all but exceptional circumstances will be catered for in mainstream schools without a statement of special educational needs (DfEE, 1994; DfEE, 1997, 1.14). That is, the consequences of dyslexia will most usually be addressed by the schools' own special educational provisions.

The working definition adopted in this report (see Sections 2.5 and 5.3) has implications for educational provision. There is, however, no ready formula to link a particular pattern or level of dyslexic difficulty to a particular formulation of learning difficulty or provision. The Code of Practice does not specify definitional features of dyslexia, but catalogues possible causal factors, aspects of curriculum difficulty, and emotional/motivational consequences, all under the umbrella of 'the child's learning difficulty' (DfEE, 1994, 3.61; Frederickson & Reason, 1995). Formulation on the matter of a learning difficulty, then, is essentially a separate, and more extensive, endeavour than formulation on the matter of dyslexia.

Since measures relating to the working definition can be norm referenced, a formulation of dyslexia may provide an indication of the degree of severity. However, as discussed in this section, local policy largely determines cut-off points regarding mild/ moderate/ severe sub-classifications of dyslexia as a special educational need. For this reason, estimates of incidence also depend on the criteria adopted.

6.3   IQ/ACHIEVEMENT DISCREPANCIES

It is possible to look for statistically unexpected contrasts between individual norm-referenced reading test scores and those predicted on the basis of IQ scores. Tables are available that show the probability of different sizes of discrepancy and the percentage of the population with discrepancies of different sizes. The use of various discrepancy criteria for the identification of dyslexia has developed in a number of local education authorities in an attempt to make the deployment of limited public resources accountable in terms of measurable cut-off points.

However, the calculation of discrepancies does not link with theoretical explanations of dyslexia (see Section 4.8). There is also doubt about the validity of IQ measures as accurate indicators of 'potential', particularly when literacy difficulties and cultural experiences can affect overall scores (for a review see Howe, 1997; Miles, 1996). Many researchers and practitioners have argued against the use of IQ/achievement discrepancies on logical, empirical, and equal opportunities grounds (see Stanovich & Stanovich, 1997). In a special edition of the journal *Dyslexia* (Vol. 2, No. 3, 1996) contributors were invited to present their current views on the discrepancy definition and, more generally, on the role of IQ in dyslexia. The contributions, from Britain (Miles, 1996), Israel (Share, 1996), Canada (Stanovich, 1996), and New Zealand (Tunmer & Chapman, 1996) were representative of the current balance of opinion in the research literature strongly weighted against the validity of discrepancy definitions.

6.4   ACCESS TO APPROPRIATE CURRICULAR OPPORTUNITIES

Considerations regarding the limitations of statistically based discrepancy definitions do not constitute arguments against the use of tests of cognitive performance *per se*. As one of the tools available to educational psychologists, standardised cognitive assessments can provide information about a child's pattern of strengths and weaknesses as well as previous learning and acquired skills (see Section 4.8). Together with other relevant educational information, the results can contribute to the planning of support for the learner in appropriate areas of learning.

The consideration of curriculum participation is an important part of educational psychology assessment. Restricted participation because of written communication difficulties will compromise curriculum breadth, balance, progression or relevance. Information can be obtained from an overview of the child's curriculum and programmes of study as well as from more direct observations that test out hypotheses about modes of curriculum presentation and student response. Account may have to be taken of the possible effects on curriculum participation resulting from a history of literacy difficulties, i.e. lost opportunities for school learning. Continuous assessment through differentiated teaching provides firmer evidence of individual requirements.

6.5   IMPLICATIONS OF THE WORKING DEFINITION FOR POLICY

The theoretical sections of the present report have demonstrated the increasing recognition of the complex interplay between cognition and emotion, biology and environment in determining literacy progress. Within this theoretical context, the purpose of educational psychology assessment is to piece together evidence from different sources in order to develop an understanding that links with plans of intervention. Knowledge about the literacy learning process is central to this endeavour. As discussed in the previous sections, however, educational assessment does not happen in isolation but depends crucially on the social policy that determines the resources that are available to education. For this reason it is important to separate out two distinct influences that interact with the working definition: first, theoretical paradigms that draw on psychological research and, second, social policy that determines educational provision. This is illustrated in Figure 6.1.

Figure 6.1 shows that the working definition may provide also a starting point for social policy decisions. The features of the definition (severity, persistence) may inform, along with research and theory about literacy learning and literacy difficulties, judgements at the Local Education Authority level regarding severe and long-term special educational needs. As suggested in Section 5.7, educational psychologists can work with schools to develop effective school-based assessment, intervention and monitoring and, within that context, also carry out detailed psychological assessment and programme planning to promote the progress of those children whose difficulties are most severe and persistent. This way of working is in accordance with the recommendations of the Green Paper, *Excellence for All Children* (DfEE, 1997).

6.6   EARLY IDENTIFICATION

The present report focuses on the assessment of school aged children. However, as described in Section 3.4, the speech and language abilities and phonological competencies of young pre-reading children can predict their subsequent reading development. The interactions between different facets of early language development are complex and, in terms of predicting later literacy, vary with age and stage of development. With regard to word reading skills, phonemic awareness and letter knowledge seem to be among the best predictors of progress (for a review see Johnston, 1998).

The wish to identify children 'at risk' is reflected in some of the commercially available tests reviewed in Appendix C. There are pitfalls, however, in identifying 'false positives' and the consequent labeling of children as having special needs or a disability. It would seem more helpful to include in the early curriculum activities that develop literacy skills such as phonological awareness and letter knowledge. Given the tools for interactive assessment and teaching that can be included in the Early Years Curriculum and the Reception Year of the National Literacy Strategy, teachers can monitor progress and notice which children continue to need help.

The Green Paper (DfEE, 1997, p.16) asks how children's special needs can be identified earlier in order to ensure that appropriate intervention addresses those needs. The term 'identification' may imply too narrow a focus on within-child determinants of learning. An alternative broader formulation would describe teachers and carers as noticing children's individual needs and then adjusting their responses accordingly. This interplay between 'noticing' and 'adjusting' would seem the most appropriate basis for monitoring the

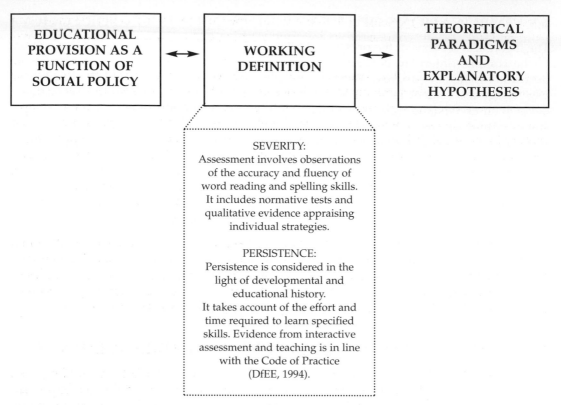

Figure 6.1: Asessing dyslexia within an educational context

progress of young children at risk of reading failure. As discussed by Reason (1998a) and Pietrowski and Reason (in press), the framework of the National Literacy Strategy provides a common approach and an agreed terminology for baseline assessments and observations that link curriculum-related assessments with teaching plans.

6.7 CULTURE-FAIR ASSESSMENT

The importance of culturally relevant contents has been emphasised in Section 3.8 of this report. If readers need both phonological and semantic information to be able to cope with all types of printed word, continuous text with a rich and varied content plays a central role in reading development. As linguistic proficiency is a pre-requisite for gaining access to meaning, children have a double disadvantage if they cannot understand the content and also struggle with orthographic representations. Dyslexia may be masked by limited mastery of the language of tuition.

According to Cline and Reason (1993), it is more than likely that the bulk of the research reviewed in the present report has been undertaken with monolingual and monocultural children. Of particular importance to practitioners in a multilingual society is research that examines the differences between children learning to read in different languages. Goswami (1997) reviews several studies involving European languages, which show that children learning in a transparent orthography will acquire spelling-sound consistencies at the phoneme level reflecting the patterns of the language. This type of information is needed for minority languages in this country in order to understand better the transfer of skills and the possible confusions arising from learning to read in different alphabetic systems.

Some research in the UK has focused on the phonological competencies of children whose home language is Sylheti or Panjabi (Frederickson & Frith, 1998; Jameson, 1996) and shown that norms developed with monolingual children are also appropriate for these groups. Studies in Canada have involved Panjabi, Tamil, Cantonese and Portugese children who have not spoken English until school entry (Geva, in press). Results obtained support those mentioned in Section 6.6: letter naming speed and phonological processing are significant predictors of word attack, word recognition and spelling skills. While differences were found between native speakers and EAL children in the area of reading comprehension, no such differences were obtained on a range of phonological tasks. It appears, therefore, that phonological difficulties can be identified in the language of tuition.

It is now fully recognised that learning difficulties of a dyslexic nature can be identified across languages, cultures, socio-economic status, race and gender. A conference entitled Multilingualism and Dyslexia, organised by the British Dyslexia Association in 1999, attracted participation from some 40 countries. A special issue of the journal *Dyslexia* (to be published early in 2000) is devoted to the key papers presented at the conference.

6.8   OLDER LEARNERS AND EXAMINATION ARRANGEMENTS

The Report of the National Working Party on Dyslexia in Higher Education (Singleton, 1998) considers whether higher education is responding adequately to the challenges represented by students with dyslexia, who may require support in order to learn and study effectively. The extensive report surveys current legislation and practice, considers issues of identification and makes recommendations with regard to policy, provision and practice.

For learners in HE direct teaching to address word reading and spelling problems usually plays a secondary role to consideration of the continuing impact of dyslexia in determining arrangements to ensure fair and equitable access to the HE curriculum. It is regarded as important to distinguish between students who struggle with the content of HE studies and students who have difficulties with written communication and associated aspects.

The issues addressed in the HE report are also relevant for pupils attending secondary school. Of particular concern are arrangements to enable access to the curriculum and examinations without 'unfair advantage over other candidates' (Joint Forum for GCSE and GCE, 1998). Woods and Reason (1999) discuss the dearth of functional information used to determine the assessment needs of individual candidates in GCSE examinations. The debate as to who can provide assessments that entitle candidates to special examination arrangements seems secondary to a consideration of what those assessments should entail.

An essential requirement would seem to be familiarity with the examination and assessment schedules of the relevant syllabuses. However, given the plethora of GCSE syllabuses (Holdstock & Radford, 1998), and assessment tiers within the syllabuses, across the full range of subjects and examination boards, the task may need some simplification. The systematic development of observation schemes or simulation exercises for extrapolation may be more viable, against general information about the range of demands for an individual candidate's particular GCSE programme.

6.9 PIECING TOGETHER THE PUZZLE

The present report gives full recognition to the plight of learners whose accurate and fluent word reading and/or spelling develops very incompletely or with great difficulty. Their dyslexia acts as a barrier to educational, social and vocational opportunities. Whatever the debates about this phenomenon, educational psychologists are committed to working in the best interests of these learners.

As has been stated in many sections of this report, the purpose of educational psychology assessment is to piece together the puzzle of dyslexia within a particular educational and social context. This involves an understanding of the literacy learning process and the reciprocal effects of educational achievements, cognitive processes, instructional circumstances and the learner's perceptions, strategies and experiences.

Having ascribed instructional circumstances a central role, educational psychology assessments draw on information obtained from teachers, parents and the learners themselves regarding the tuition provided and the learner's developmental and educational history. Educational psychologists can then become involved in the design and monitoring of learning programmes and give advice about teaching in general and individual instructional approaches in particular (Code of Practice, DfEE, 1994).

It may be that, at a particular time, sufficient evidence or assessment information is not available or it may be that other terminology provides a better overall description of the child's difficulties. As the working definition in this report focuses on accurate and fluent word reading and spelling, the psychologist will consider whether there are other areas of concern for the child, extending beyond the working definition, which will need to be addressed and which may suggest a better fit with some other descriptor(s).

Requests for clarification of the connection between a child's learning difficulty and dyslexia is often made in the form of the question 'is this child's dyslexia severe enough to warrant additional special educational provision, i.e. to constitute a marked special educational need?' As outlined in Sections 6.1 and 6.2, there is no simple answer to this question. The reply depends not only on the appraisal of the child's curriculum participation but the range of provision available within a school/local authority. Foremost is the consideration of whether the provision made is appropriate.

CONCLUSIONS

✦ At a national level, the continuum of special educational needs is defined in relation to special educational provision. It allows for variation in the manifestation of special educational needs since what provision is considered to be special may vary between teachers, schools and Local Education Authorities.

✦ The resultant fluidity in constructions of special educational needs leads some theorists to question the validity and utility of the concept. They prefer instead to focus on the effects of curriculum and school organisation in accommodating the whole variety of students' individual educational needs.

✦ Local policy largely determines cut-off points regarding mild/moderate/severe sub-classifications of dyslexia as a special educational need. For this reason, estimates of incidence also depend on the criteria adopted.

✦ Statistically unexpected contrasts between individual norm-referenced reading test scores and those predicted on the basis of IQ scores (discrepancy criteria of dyslexia) can be criticised on theoretical grounds.

✦ The consideration of access to appropriate curricular opportunities is an important part of educational psychology assessment. Information can be obtained from an overview of the child's curriculum and programmes of study as well as from more direct observations that test out hypotheses about modes of curriculum presentation and student response.

✦ The working definition adopted in this report can also provide a starting point for social policy decisions. The features of the definition (severity, persistence) may inform, along with research and theory about literacy learning and literacy difficulties, judgements at the Local Education Authority level regarding severe and long-term special educational needs.

✦ Educational psychologists work with schools to develop effective school-based assessment, intervention and monitoring and, within that context, also carry out detailed psychological assessment and programme planning to promote the progress of those children whose difficulties are most severe and persistent.

✦ With regard to early identification, educational psychologists can help teachers and carers to *notice* children's individual needs and then *adjust* their responses accordingly. Given the tools for interactive assessment and teaching that can be included in the Early Years Curriculum and the Reception Year of the National Literacy Strategy, it is possible to monitor progress in early literacy learning and to notice which children continue to need help.

✦ Culture-fair assessment requires that learning difficulties of a dyslexic nature are identified across languages, cultures, socio-economic status, race and gender. Even when the learner's home language is not English, research has shown that phonological difficulties, as one important determinant of literacy, can be identified in the language of tuition.

✦ For older learners direct teaching to address word reading and spelling problems usually plays a secondary role to consideration of the continuing impact of dyslexia in determining arrangements to ensure fair and equitable access to the curriculum and examination arrangements.

✦ The purpose of educational psychology assessment is to piece together the puzzle of dyslexia within a particular educational and social context. This involves an understanding of the literacy learning process and the reciprocal effects of educational achievements, cognitive processes, instructional circumstances and the learner's perceptions, strategies and experiences. To be useful, the assessment needs to lead to workable plans of action that promote learning.

Section 7: OVERALL CONCLUSIONS

1.   THE SCOPE OF THE REPORT

1.1   The remit of the Working Party was to write a brief report to clarify the current concept of dyslexia, its links with literacy learning/difficulties and implications for educational psychology assessment and intervention. While children of primary school age proved to be the main focus of the report, it has implications beyond that age range.

1.2   The report reviews relevant research in the area of dyslexia and special needs. It draws on a survey of current educational psychology practice and extensive consultation based on a draft report. It builds on a previous national enquiry instigated by the DECP and is designed to complement the DECP guidance for educational psychology assessment in general. It is in full accordance with The British Psychological Society Code of Conduct for Psychologists.

1.3   The report considers the concept of dyslexia in relation to relevant educational legislation and links with the Code of Practice on the identification and assessment of special educational need (DfEE, 1994), the subsequent Green Paper (DfEE, 1997) and current consultations regarding the development of special education practices.

2.   A WORKING DEFINITION OF DYSLEXIA

2.1   In cognitive psychology 'dyslexia' has for many years been a short-hand for marked difficulty with the alphabetic script. The term has now entered the realms of popular language and also requires consideration from a social psychological standpoint. There has been a tendency to avoid the term in educational practice because of its predominant emphasis on within-child causative factors rather than effective teaching and inclusive practices.

2.2   To clarify the concept of dyslexia, there is a need to start with a working definition that separates description from causal explanations. The following working definition is adopted in the present report: *Dyslexia is evident when accurate and fluent word reading and/or spelling develops very incompletely or with great difficulty. This focuses on literacy learning at the 'word level' and implies that the problem is severe and persistent despite appropriate learning opportunities. It provides the basis for a staged process of assessment through teaching.*

2.3   In terms of the National Literacy Strategy (DfEE, 1998), dyslexia can be defined as marked and persistent problems at the word level of the NLS curricular framework. As such, it leads to the evaluation of learning opportunities and teaching methods introduced within a mainstream educational setting.

2.4   The working definition provides a starting point for generating and testing a broad range of hypotheses that draw on psychological theory and research linked to different causal explanations. At the individual level, this approach encompasses multivariate explanations rather than a search for single causative factors.

2.5   The working definition has no exclusionary criteria. Positive identifying characteristics focus in the first instance on severe and persistent problems with accurate/fluent word recognition and spelling, and take priority over other factors including overall ability, linguistic and cultural background.

2.6   In focusing on the quantification and understanding of literacy difficulties, the working definition is not synonymous with specific learning difficulties. Nevertheless, it can provide a starting point for assessing the extent to which literacy difficulties are leading to special educational needs that hinder appropriate access to relevant areas of the curriculum.

3.   LITERACY LEARNING AND DYSLEXIA

3.1   The report considers difficulties in learning to read and spell in the context of current knowledge of skilled performance and of the way that literacy skills are acquired by young learners.

3.2   Word reading involves rapid and automatic mapping of letter strings on to the most likely pronunciation. Skilled spelling also involves an implicit knowledge of the probabilities of particular letter patterns occurring together.

3.3   The speech and language abilities and phonological competencies of young pre-reading children can predict their subsequent reading development. The interactions between different facets of early language development are complex and, in terms of predicting later literacy, vary with age and stage of development.

3.4   According to current research, phonological coding provides a central unifying thread in the word reading process. However, the role, amount and relative weight of phonological processing, and how complete this has to be, is likely to alter in the course of reading development.

3.5   Skilled and fluent readers make little use of contextual clues in word reading other than to clarify the intended meaning when the same spelling has more than one possible meaning. Unlike fluent readers, poor readers require contextual information as a compensatory strategy in assisting word recognition.

3.6   The whole language model of reading conceives word reading as a 'psycho-linguistic guessing game'. It is argued that, driven by a search for meaning, the fluent reader makes educated guesses on the basis of the text already read. A crucial assumption is that most words can be 'read' as wholes, visually. The evidence against such an account of reading behaviour is by now incontrovertible. Accurate and fluent word decoding is a pre-requisite for efficient reading for interest and information.

3.7   Stage models of the development of word reading and spelling are not only of interest in research but also relevant to educational practitioners. The mechanisms involved in the transition from one stage to the next are, however, not specified. Reading development is dependent on the teaching methods deployed, and, also, the language in which children are learning to read.

3.8   The amount, type and breadth of reading that learners undertake is crucial to their reading development via a process of self teaching. Motivation and interest, therefore, become important as do semantic and syntactic abilities integral to the self-teaching process. Nevertheless, phonological recoding is crucial in self-teaching, and thus the efficiency and integrity of underlying phonological abilities will determine how effectively children are able to learn through independent reading.

3.9   According to a 'connectionist' framework, learners need both phonological and semantic information to be able to read all types of printed word. The framework can incorporate different areas and levels of difficulty in terms of continuous variation in underlying skills as they interact with the environment. Dyslexia can then be regarded as a function of the reciprocal effects of learning opportunities and the type and extent of phonological and semantic strengths and difficulties.

3.10   Accounts of skilled performance and of how children become skilled readers allow practitioners to put the assessment and intervention required into a useful context. The starting point is an analysis of children's reading and spelling performances, their learning experiences and their weaknesses in phonological processing and representational abilities. Within this context the question of whether a child is dyslexic or not may then be addressed.

4.   THEORETICAL EXPLANATIONS

4.1   The purpose of the theoretical section is to inform practitioners of research and theory in the area of dyslexia. The term 'hypothesis' is, therefore, used in relation to different theoretical approaches developed by academic researchers to explain the concept of dyslexia. Implications with regard to hypotheses formulated in educational psychology assessment and intervention are considered separately in Sections 5 and 6.

4.2   The working definition introduced in Section 2.5 provides a starting point for the present review of different theoretical approaches and their research basis. Each approach is considered within a causal modelling framework involving three levels of analysis: the biological (brain), the cognitive and the behavioural.

4.3   Some of the theoretical accounts of dyslexia include comprehensive description at each level in the framework and, in addition, model causal links between the features included at different levels. It is important to consider the extent to which available empirical evidence suggests that these should be regarded as alternative accounts of a unitary construct of 'dyslexia', as opposed to being regarded as accounts of different types of dyslexia.

4.4   The phonological deficit/delay hypothesis provides the main focus, both because of the broad empirical support that it commands and because of the role phonology is accorded in many of the other hypotheses in mediating the impact of dyslexia on the acquisition of word reading and spelling skills. The following hypotheses include phonological processing as a major component:

-   the temporal order hypothesis that focuses on the speed of processing required in integrating speech and non-speech stimuli.

-   the skill automatisation hypothesis which proposes that underlying brain mechanisms affect a range of tasks requiring rapid and automatic processing.

-   the working memory hypothesis which postulates particular difficulties in processing and storing information that is linguistically coded.

4.5   The syndrome hypothesis and the core phonological deficit/delay hypothesis have more in common than may have been recognised. Both hypotheses reject exclusionary criteria and look for positive indicators, including phonological processing and memory. Both acknowledge that particular literacy problems can occur in children of all levels of cognitive ability. Both can examine associated difficulties, whether cognitive or emotional, in order to specify individual educational needs.

4.6   While current research has focused on dyslexia as a language problem, there is continuing interest in many aspects of visual processing. However, measures such as visual sequential memory or visual matching, previously regarded as tapping relevant visual processes, seem to play no part in current research literature. Present rationales and methods involve much greater sophistication, including complex technology and accurate timing.

4.7   The validity of identifying dyslexia in terms of statistically unexpected contrasts between actual literacy attainments and those predicted on the grounds of IQ scores, is not supported by the body of evidence showing that children of different IQ levels perform similarly on a variety of measures of reading and spelling.

4.8   Profiles of test scores obtained from batteries of tests designed to assess cognitive performance (e.g. the BAS and the WISC) can aid understanding of the learners particular strengths and weaknesses. No particular cognitive profile, however, can adequately discriminate between children with or without literacy difficulties of a dyslexic nature. Furthermore, it is important to consider the validity and reliability of test results in relation to children's cultural experiences and life events.

4.9   Research on subtypes of dyslexia is inconclusive. Much of the work has not been grounded in current theories of cognitive processing. In cognitive research, the debate contrasts dual-route models (involving visual and phonological pathways to the semantic system) with models in which the degree of phonological difficulty accounts for different types/levels of word reading and spelling difficulty. There is agreement, however, that dimensions of individual differences in dyslexia are more important than discrete subtypes.

4.10   Learning opportunities and social context hypotheses are based on the assumption that differences in literacy skills performance between children result primarily from differences between them in learning opportunities and experiences, rather than inherent differences. It seems more appropriate, however, to consider the interaction between learning experiences and individual differences in producing different patterns of performance.

4.11   Emotional difficulties can be associated with dyslexia. Whist these affective responses are not the causes, but rather the consequences, of dyslexia, they may contribute to and exacerbate learning difficulties in a complex and incremental way.

5.   IMPLICATIONS FOR EDUCATIONAL PSYCHOLOGY ASSESSMENT AND INTERVENTION

5.1   While focusing primarily on word reading and spelling, the present report is located within a wider framework for psychological assessment and intervention that involves all relevant areas of experience and learning.

5.2   The working definition adopted in this report requires that three aspects be evaluated through the assessment process:

-     that the pupil is learning/has learnt accurate and fluent word reading and/or spelling very incompletely;

-     that appropriate learning opportunities have been provided;

– that progress has been made only as a result of much additional effort/instruction and that difficulties have, nevertheless, persisted.

5.3 With increased knowledge of learning and literacy difficulties in the primary school, it is assumed that monitored intervention can take place early enough to ensure that the process of interactive assessment and teaching does not result in any unnecessary delay for those learners with severe and persistent difficulties. Nevertheless, there may be instances where personal and educational circumstances are such that the persistence of difficulties will need to be ascertained in more indirect ways.

5.4 The accuracy and fluency of word reading and spelling can be assessed normatively through standardised tests and informally through a series of literacy related tasks that reflect the teaching that has taken place.

5.5 The conclusion that the acquisition of reading and spelling is 'very incomplete' depends on the age and developmental stage of the learner. It triggers an investigation of factors that may be important in understanding the nature of the difficulties being experienced and in identifying ways of overcoming or alleviating them.

5.6 Appendix C evaluates a selection of commercially available tests designed to assess cognitive processes associated with dyslexia. The evaluations demonstrate that no one test can be considered obligatory in educational psychology assessments.

5.7 Several tests have been developed for the purposes of tapping phonological competencies and are useful when interpreted in the light of the learners' experiences of literacy and the instruction received. The assessment of visual processes is complicated by the fact that simple memory of visual patterns, as introduced in earlier tests, appears to be of no relevance.

5.8 Assessments referring to cognitive test scores within batteries of tests, such as the BAS and WISC, can be informative when pointing to strengths and weaknesses in the individual case. No particular pattern of sub-test scores, however, can be regarded as necessary or sufficient in deciding whether and to what extent learning difficulties can be described as dyslexic.

5.9 In assessing overall learning opportunities, psychologists can draw on a range of research that describes the characteristics of effective instruction.

5.10 In the context of the National Literacy Strategy, dyslexia can be defined as marked and persistent problems at the word level of the framework. With explicit guidance on 'assessing to teach' and the principles and practices of 'mastery learning' the framework provides a good basis for developing inclusive practices.

5.11 The evaluation of persistence in the light of response to additional teaching can involve the monitoring of rate of learning progress through methods such as single-subject experimental research and precision teaching. These methods offer a set of strategies for carrying out focused assessments of pupil performance over time and for recording progress in a way that facilitates judgements about accuracy and fluency of performance.

5.12 The information considered in this section can be conceptualised as a network of reciprocal effects involving literacy performance, hypotheses about underlying processes and appraisal of learning opportunities and teaching methods.

6. SPECIAL EDUCATIONAL NEEDS AND DYSLEXIA

6.1   At a national level, the continuum of special educational needs is defined in relation to special educational provision. It allows for variation in the manifestation of special educational needs since what provision is considered to be special may vary between teachers, schools and Local Education Authorities.

6.2   The resultant fluidity in constructions of special educational needs leads some theorists to question the validity and utility of the concept. They prefer instead to focus on the effects of curriculum and school organisation in accommodating the whole variety of students' individual educational needs.

6.3   Local policy largely determines cut-off points regarding mild/moderate/severe sub-classifications of dyslexia as a special educational need. For this reason, estimates of incidence also depend on the criteria adopted.

6.4   Statistically unexpected contrasts between individual norm-referenced reading test scores and those predicted on the basis of IQ scores (discrepancy criteria of dyslexia) can be criticised on theoretical grounds.

6.5   The consideration of access to appropriate curricular opportunities is an important part of educational psychology assessment. Information can be obtained from an overview of the child's curriculum and programmes of study as well as from more direct observations that test out hypotheses about modes of curriculum presentation and student response.

6.6   The working definition adopted in this report can also provide a starting point for social policy decisions. The features of the definition (severity, persistence) may inform, along with research and theory about literacy learning and literacy difficulties, judgements at the Local Education Authority level regarding severe and long-term special educational needs.

6.7   Educational psychologists work with schools to develop effective school-based assessment, intervention and monitoring and, within that context, also carry out detailed psychological assessment and programme planning to promote the progress of those children whose difficulties are most severe and persistent.

6.8   With regard to early identification, educational psychologists can help teachers and carers to *notice* children's individual needs and then adjust their responses accordingly. Given the tools for interactive assessment and teaching that can be included in the Early Years Curriculum and the Reception Year of the National Literacy Strategy, it is possible to monitor progress in early literacy learning and to notice which children continue to need help.

6.9   Culture-fair assessment requires that learning difficulties of a dyslexic nature are identified across languages, cultures, socio-economic status, race and gender. Even when the learner's home language is not English, research has shown that phonological difficulties, as one important determinant of literacy, can be identified in the language of tuition.

6.10   For older learners direct teaching to address word reading and spelling problems usually plays a secondary role to consideration of the continuing impact of dyslexia in determining arrangements to ensure fair and equitable access to the curriculum and examination arrangements.

6.11   The purpose of educational psychology assessment is to piece together the puzzle of dyslexia within a particular educational and social context. This involves an understanding of the literacy learning process and the reciprocal effects of educational achievements, cognitive processes, instructional circumstances and the learner's perceptions, strategies and experiences. To be useful, the assessment needs to lead to workable plans of action that promote learning.

REFERENCES

Ackerman, D. & Howes, C. (1986). Sociometric status and after-school activity of children with learning disabilities. *Journal of Learning Disabilities, 2,* 416-419.

Adelman, H.S. (1989). Beyond the learning mystique: an interactional perspective on learning disabilities. *Journal of Learning Disabilities, 22,* 5, 301-304.

Adams, M.J. (1990). *Beginning to Read: Children Thinking and Learning about Print.* Cambridge, Mass: MIT Press.

Adams, M.J. (1993). Beginning to read: An Overview. In R. Beard (Ed.) *Teaching Literacy: Balancing Perspectives.* London: Hodder & Stoughton.

Ainscow, M. (Ed.) (1991). *Effective Schools for All.* London: David Fulton.

Ainscow, M. (1998). Exploring links between special needs and school improvement. *Support for Learning, 13,* 2, 70-75.

Ames, C. & Archer, J. (1988). Achievement goals in the classroom: Students' learning strategies and motivation processes. *Journal of Educational Psychology, 80,* 3, 260-267.

Armstrong, D. (1995). *Power and Partnership in Education.* London: Routledge.

Association of Educational Psychologists (1998). *Guidance to Educational Psychologists in Preparing Statutory Advice to the L.E.A.* Durham: AEP.

Audit Commission (1992). Getting in on the Act. Provision for pupils with special educational needs: The national picture. London: HMSO.

Baddeley, A.D. (1986). *Working Memory.* London: Oxford University Press.

Balota, D.A. & Rayner, K. (1991). Word recognition processes in foveal and parafoveal vision: The range of influence of lexical variables. In D. Besner & G.W. Humphries (Eds.) *Basic Processes in Reading: Visual Word Recognition.* London: Lawrence Erlbaum.

Bakker, D.J.(1979). Hemispheric differences and reading strategies : two dyslexias?, *Bulletin of the Orton Society, 29,* 84-100.

Barton, L. (Ed) (1988). *The Politics of special educational needs.* London: Falmer Press.

Beard, R. (1999). *National Literacy Strategy: Review of Research and other Related Evidence.* Sudbury, Suffolk: DfEE Publications

Besner, D. & Humphries, G.W. (Eds.) (1991). *Basic Processes in Reading: Visual Word Recognition.* London: Lawrence Erlbaum.

Biggar, S. & Barr, J. (1996). The emotional world of specific learning difficulties. In G. Reid (Ed.) *Dimensions of Dyslexia Vol 2.* Edinburgh: Moray House.

Blachman, B. (Ed.) (1997). *Foundations of Reading Acquisition and Dyslexia.* London: Lawrence Erlbaum.

Boder, E. (1973). Developmental dyslexia: a diagnostic approach based on three atypical reading patterns. *Developmental Medicine and Child Neurology, 15,* 663-87.

Booth, T. (1994). Continua or chimera? *British Journal of Special Education, 21,* 1, 21-24.

Booth, S. R. & Jay, M. (1981). The use of precision teaching technology in the work of the educational psychologist. *Journal of the Association of Educational Psychologists, 5,* 5, 21-26.

Booth S.R. & Jewell, T. (1983). Programmes for slow learners. *Journal of the Association of Educational Psychologists, 6* (2), 58-62.

Brady, S. & Shankweiler, D. (1991). *Phonological Processes in Literacy.* New Jersey: Lawrence Erlbaum.

Brenna, B. (1995). The metacognitive reading strategies of five early readers. *Journal of Research in Reading, 18,* 1, 53-62.

British Psychological Society (1994). *Code of Conduct for Psychologists.* Leicester: The BPS.

Brown, P. (1996). Metacognition in reading. In G. Reid (Ed.) *Dimensions of Dyslexia Vol 2: Literacy, Language and Learning.* Edinburgh: Moray House.

Butkowski, I.S. & Willows, D.M. (1980). Cognitive-motivational characteristics of children varying in reading ability: Evidence for learned helplessness in poor readers. *Journal of Educational Psychology, 72,* 3, 408-422.

Cain, K. & Oakhill, J. (1998). Comprehension skill and inference-making ability: Issues and causality. In C. Hulme & R. M. Joshi (Eds.) *Reading and Spelling: Development and Disorders.* London: Lawrence Erlbaum.

Cardon, L.R., Smith, S.D., Fulker, D.W., Kimberling, W.J., Pennington, B.F. & DeFries, J.C. (1994). Quantitative trait locus for reading disability on chromosome 6. *Science, 226,* 276-279.

Casey, R., Levy, S.E., Brown, K. & Brooks-Gunn, J. (1992). Impaired emotional health in children with mild reading disability. *Developmental and Behavioural Paediatrics, 13,* 4, 256-260.

Castles, A. & Coltheart, M. (1993). Varieties of developmental dyslexia. *Cognition, 47,* 149-180.

Chasty, H. & Friel, J. (1991). *Children with Special Needs: Assessment, Law and Practice.* London: Jessica Kingsley.

Cline, T. & Reason, R. (1993). Specific learning difficulties (dyslexia): Equal opportunities issues. *British Journal of Special Education, Research Section, 20,* 1, 30-34.

Coles, G.S. (1989) Excerpts from the learning mystique: a critical look at learning disabilities. *Journal of Learning Disabilitiess, 22,* 5, 267-277.

Coltheart, M. & Jackson, N.E. (1998). Defining Dyslexia. *Child Psychology and Psychiatry Review, 3* (1), 12-16.

Connor, M. (1994). Specific learning difficulties (dyslexia) and interventions. *Support for Learning, 9,* 3, 114-119.

Cook, J. (1999). Reading and spelling tests. *Educational Psychology in Practice, 15,* 1, 9-19.

Cornelissen, P., Bradley, L., Fowler, M.S. & Stein, J.F. (1992). Covering one eye affects how some children read. *Developmental Medicine and Child Neurology, 34,* 296-304.

Cornwall, A. & Bawden, H.N. (1992). Reading disabilities and aggression: A critical review. *Journal of Learning.Disabilities, 25,* 5, 281-288.

Darke, S. (1988) Anxiety and working memory capacity. *Cognition and Emotion, 2,* 145-154.

DeFries, J.C., Alarcon, M. & Olson, R.K.(1997). Genetic aetiologies if reading and spelling difficulties. In C. Hulme and M. Snowling (Eds.) *Dyslexia: Biology, Cognition and Intervention.* London: Whurr.

Department for Education (1981). *The Education Act 1981.* London: HMSO.

Department for Education (1989). *Circular 22/89.* London: HMSO.

Department for Education and Employment (1994). *Code of Practice on the Identification and Assessment of Special Educational Needs.* London: HMSO.

Department for Education and Employment (1996). *The Education Act 1996.* London: HMSO.

Department for Education and Employment (1997). *Excellence for All Children: Meeting Special Educational Needs (Green Paper).* London: HMSO.

Department for Education and Employment (1998). *The National Literacy Strategy Framework for Teaching.* London: HMSO.

Dodds, J. (1994). Spelling skills and causal attribution in children. *Educational Psychology in Practice, 10,* 2, 111-119.

Duncan, L.G., Seymour, P.H.K. & Hill, S. (1997). How important are rhyme and analogy in beginning reading? *Cognition, 63,* 171-208.

Dunlop, P. (1972). Dyslexia: Then orthoptic approach. *Australian Journal of Orthoptics, 12,* 16-20

Dyson, A. (1994). Towards a collaborative learning model for responding to student diversity. *Support for Learning, 9,* 2, 53-60.

Eden, G.F., VanMeter, J.W., Rumsey, J.M., Maisog, J.M., Woods, R.P. & Zeffiro, T.A. (1996). Abnormal processing of visual motion in dyslexia revealed by functional brain imaging. *Nature, 382,* 66-69.

Edwards, J. (1994). *The Scars of Dyslexia.* London: Cassell.

Elliott, C.D. (1998). Reply 1 in Reactions to 'Understanding and managing dyslexia'. Letter to *The British Psychological Society Division of Educational and Child Psychology Newsletter, 84,* 43-45.

Elliott, C.D., Smith, P. & McCulloch, K.(1996). *British Ability Scales II.* Windsor: NFER-Nelson.

Ellis, A.W., McDougall, S.J.P. & Monk, A.F. (1996a). Are dyslexics different? I. A comparison between dyslexics, reading age controls, poor readers and precocious readers. *Dyslexia, 2,* 31-58.

Ellis, A.W., McDougall, S.J.P. & Monk, A.F. (1996b). Are dyslexics different? II. Individual differences among dyslexics, reading age controls, poor readers and precocious readers. *Dyslexia, 2,* 59-68.

Evans, B.J.W. (1997). Assessment of visual problems in reading. In J.R. Beech and C. Singleton (Eds.) *The Psychological Assessment of Reading.* London: Routledge.

Evans, B.J.W. & Drasdo, N. (1991). Tinted lenses and related therapies for learning disabilities: A review. *Opthalmic and Physiological Optics, 11,* 206-217.

Fairhurst, P. & Pumfrey, P.D. (1992). Secondary school organisation and the self concepts of pupils with relative reading difficulties. *Research in Education, 47,* 17-28.

Faludy, T. & Faludy, A. (1996). *A Little Edge of Darkness: A Boy's Triumph over Dyslexia.* London: Jessica Kingsley.

Farmer, M.E. and Klein, R. (1995). The evidence for a temporal processing deficit linked to dyslexia: A review. *Psychonomic Bulletin and Review, 2,* 4, 460-493.

Farmer, T.W., Pearl, R. & Van Acker, R.M. (1996). Expanding the social skills defect framework: A developmental synthesis perspective, classroom social networks and implications for the social growth of students with disabilities. *Journal of Special Education, 30, 3,* 232-256.

Faupel, A. (1986). Curriculum management (part 2): Teaching curriculum objectives. *Educational Psychology in Practice, 2, 2,* 4-15.

Fawcett, A., & Nicolson, R. (Eds.) (1994). *Dyslexia in Children: Multi-disciplinary Perspectives.* London: Harvester Wheatsheaf.

Felton, R.H. & Wood, F.B. (1992). A reading level match study of non-word reading skills in poor readers with varying IQs. *Journal of Learning Disabilities, 25, 5,* 318-326

Fisher, R. (1998). Thinking about thinking: Developing metacognition in children. *Early Child Development and Care, 141,* 1-13.

Flowers, D. L. (1993). Brain Basis for Dyslexia : A summary of work in progress. *Journal of Learning Disabilities, 26, 9,* 575-582.

Flynn, J.M., Deering, W., Goldstein, M. & Rahbar, M.H. (1992). Electrophysiological correlates of dyslexia subtypes. *Journal of Learning Disabilities, 25, 2,* 133-141.

Folk, J.R. & Morris, R.K. (1995). Multiple Lexical Codes in Reading: Evidence from Eye Movements, Naming Times, and Oral Reading. *Journal of Experimental Psychology: Learning, Memory and Cognition, 21* (6), 1412-1429.

Frederickson, N. (1999). The ACID test – or is it? *Educational Psychology in Practice, 15,* 1, 2-8.

Frederickson, N. & Frith, U. (1998). Identifying dyslexia in bilingual children: A phonological approach with Inner London Sylheti speakers. *Dyslexia, 4,* 119-131.

Frederickson, N. & Monsen, J. (1999). The learning environment. In Cameron, R.J. & Frederickson, N. (Eds.) *Psychology in Education Portfolio.* Windsor: NFER-Nelson.

Frederickson, N. & Reason, R. (1995). Discrepancy definitions of specific learning difficulties. *Educational Psychology in Practice, 10, 4,* 195-206.

Friedman, G. & Stevenson, J. (1988). Reading processes in specific reading retarded and reading backward 13-year-olds. *British Journal of Developmental Psychology, 6,* 97-108

Frith, U. (1985). Beneath the surface of developmental dyslexia. In K. Patterson, M. Coltheart & J. Marshall (Eds.) *Surface Dyslexia.* London: Routledge and Kegan Paul.

Frith, U. (1995). Dyslexia: Can we have a shared theoretical framework? *Educational and Child Psychology, 12,* 1, 6-17.

Frith, U. (1997). Brain, mind and behaviour in dyslexia. In C. Hulme & M. Snowling (Eds.) *Dyslexia: Biology, Cognition and Intervention.* London: Whurr.

Galaburda, A.M. (1989). Ordinary and extraordinary brain development: Anatomical variation in development dyslexia. *Annals of Dyslexia, 39,* 67-79.

Galaburda, A.M. (1993). *Dyslexia and Development: Neurobiological Aspects of Extra-Ordinary Brains.* Cambridge, MA: Harvard University Press.

Galaburda, A.M. (1993). Developmental dyslexia and animal studies: at the interface between cognition and neurology. In A.M. Galaburda (Ed.) *Dyslexia and Development : Neurobiological Aspects of Extra-ordinary Brains.* Cambridge, MA : Harvard University Press.

Galaburda, A.M. & Livingstone, M. (1993). Evidence for a magnocellular defect in developmental dyslexia. In P. Tallal, A.M. Galaburda, R.R. Limas & C. von Euler (Eds.) *Temporal Information Processing in the Nervous System: Specia Reference to Dyslexia and Dysphasia* (pp.70-82). New York: The New York Academy of Sciences.

Gardner, H. (1984). *Frames of Mind: The Theory of Multiple Intelligences.* London: Heinemann.

Gentile, L.M. & McMillan, M.M. (1987). *Stress and Reading Difficulties: Research Assessment and Intervention.* Newark, DE: International Reading Association.

Gersons-Wolfensberger, D.C.M. & Ruijssenaars, W.A.J.J.M. (1997). Definition and treatment of dyslexia: A report by the Committee on Dyslexia of the Health Council of the Netherlands. *Journal of Learning Disabilities, 30,* 2, 209-213.

Geva, E. (in press). Issues in the assessment of reading disabilities in L2 children – beliefs and research evidence. *Dyslexia: An International Journal of Research and Practice, 6,* 1.

Gibbs, S. (1998). Lexical knowledge, memory, phonological awareness and word reading: Towards a statistical model. *Technical Report No 55.* Nottingham University: Department of Psychology ESRC Centre for Research in Development, Instruction and Training.

Gjessing, H.J. & Karlsen, B. (1989). *A Longitudinal Study of Dyslexia.* New York: Springer Verlag.

Goodman, K.S. & Goodman, Y.M. (1977). Learning about psycholinguistic processing by analysing oral reading. *Harvard Educational Review, 47,* 3, 317-332.

Goswami, U. (1997). Learning to read in different orthographies: Phonological awareness, orthographic representations and dyslexia. In C. Hulme and M. Snowling (Eds.) *Dyslexia: Biology, Cognition and Intervention.* London: Whurr.

Goswami, U. & Bryant, P.E. (1990). *Phonological Skills and Learning to Read.* London: Lawrence Erlbaum.

Gough, P.B. Ehri, L.C. and Treiman, R. (Eds.) (1992). *Reading Acquisition.* London: Lawrence Erlbaum.

Goulandris, N., McIntyre, A., Snowling, M., Bethel, J. & Lee, J.P. (1998). A comparison of dyslexic and normal readers using orthoptic assessment procedures. *Dyslexia, 4,* 30-48.

Goulandris, N. & Snowling, M. (1991). Visual memory deficits: A plausible cause of developmental dyslexia. Evidence from a single case study. *Cognitive Neuropsychology, 8,* 127-154.

Greaney, J. & Reason, R. (1999). Phonological processing in Braille. *Dyslexia: An International Journal of Research and Practice, 5,* 4, p.8-20.

Greaney, K.T., Tunmer, W.E. & Chapman, J.W. (1997). Effects of Rime-Based Orthographic Analogy Training on the Word Recognition Skills of Children With Reading Disability. *Journal of Educational Psychology, 89,* 4, 645-651.

Hampshire, S. (1990). *Susan's Story.* London: Corgi.

Hanley, J.R., Reynolds, C.J. & Thornton, A. (1997). Orthographic analogies and developmental dyslexia. *British Journal of Psychology, 88,* 423-440.

Hasbrouck, J.E., Woldbeck, T., Ihnot, C. & Parker, R.I. (1999). One teachers's use of curriculum-based measurement: A changed opinion. *Learning Disabilities Research and Practice, 14,* 2, 118-126.

Hatcher, P., Hulme, C. & Ellis, A. (1994). Ameliorating early reading failure by integrating the teaching of reading with phonological skills. *Child Development, 65,* 41-57.

Hempel, C.G. (1966). *Philosophy of Natural Science.* Englewood Cliffs, NJ: Prentice-Hall.

Hinshaw, S.P. (1992). Externalising behaviour problems and academic under-achievement in childhood and adolescence. *Psychological Bulletin, 111,* 127-155.

Hogben, J.H. (1997). How does visual transient deficit affect reading? In C. Hulme and M. Snowling (Eds.) *Dyslexia: Biology, Cognition and Intervention.* London: Whurr.

Hoien, T., Lundberg, I., Stanovich, K.E. & Bjaalid, I.K. (1995). Components of Phonological Awareness. *Reading and Writing: an Interdisciplinary Journal. 7,* 171-188.

Holdstock, L. & Radford, J. (1998). Psychology passes its 1997 exams. *The Psychologist, 11, 3,* 117-119.

Howe, M.A.J. (1997). *IQ in Question: The Truth about Intelligence.* London: Sage.

Hugdahl, K. (1993). Functional Brain Asymmetry, Dyslexia and Immune Disorders. In A.M. Galaburda (Ed.) *Dyslexia and development: Neurobiological Aspects of Extra-Ordinary Brains.* Cambridge, MA: Harvard University Press.

Hulme, C. & Joshi, R.M. (1998). *Reading and Spelling: Development and Disorders.* London: Lawrence Erlbaum.

Hulme, C. & Roodenrys, S. (1995). Verbal working memory development and its disorders. *Journal of Child Psychology and Psychiatry, 36, 3,* 373-398.

Hulme, C. & Snowling, M. (Eds.) (1997). *Dyslexia: Biology, Cognition, and Intervention.* London. Whurr.

Huntington, D.D. & Bender, W.D. (1993). Adolescents with learning disabilities at risk? Emotional well being, depression and suicide. *Journal of Learning Disabilities, 26,* 159-166.

Hynd, G.W. (1992). Neurological aspects of dyslexia: comment on the balance model, *Journal of Learning Disabilities, 25, 2,* 110-111.

Hynd, G.W. & Hiemenz, J.R. (1997). Dyslexia and gyral morphology variation. In C. Hulme & M. Snowling (Eds.) *Dyslexia: Biology, cognition and Intervention.* London : Whurr.

Innes, P. (1991). *Defeating Dyslexia: A Boy's Story.* London: Kyle Cathie.

Irwin, D.E. (1998). Lexical Processing during Saccadic Eye Movements. *Cognitive Psychology 36,* 1-27.

Jameson, S. (1996). Phonological awareness in bilingual children. University of Manchester: *Unpublished MSc thesis.*

Johnston, R.S. (1998). The case for orthographic knowledge. *Journal of Research in Reading, 21, 3,* 195-200.

Joint forum for GCSE and GCE (1998). *Candidates with Special Assessment Needs.* Manchester: NEAB.

Jorm, A.F., Share, D.L., Maclean, R. & Matthews, R. (1986). Cognitive factors at school entry predictive of specific reading retardation and general reading backwardness. *Journal of Child Psychology and Psychiatry, 27,* 45-54.

Karmiloff-Smith, A. (1997). Crucial differences between developmental cognitive neuroscience and adult neuropsychology. *Neurological Neuropsychology, 13,* 513-524.

Kaufman, A.S. (1994) *Intelligent Testing with the WISC-III.* New York: Wiley.

Kavale, K.A. & Forness, S.R. (1996). Social skills deficits and learning disabilities: A meta-analysis. *Journal of Learning Disabilities, 29, 3,* 226-237.

Kessissoglou, S. & Farrell, P. (1995). Whatever happened to precision teaching. *British Journal of Special Education, 22, 2,* 60-63.

Kulik, J.A. (1991). Mastering Learning. Chapter 4 in K.A. Spencer (Ed.) *The Psychology of Educational Technology and Instructional Media.* Liverpool: Manutius Press.

Lazarus, R.S. & Smith, C.A. (1988). Knowledge and appraisal in the cognition-emotional relationship. *Cognition and Emotion, 2,* 281-300.

Lazo, M.G. Pumfrey, P.D. & Peers, I. (1997). Metalinguistic awareness, reading and spelling: Roots and branches in literacy. *Journal of Research in Reading, 20,* 2, 85-104.

Licht, R. & Spyer, G. (Eds.) (1994). *The Balance Model of Dyslexia.* Assen: Van Gorcum.

Linsley, O.R. (1992). Precision teaching: Discoveries and effects. *Journal of Applied Behaviour Analysis, 25,* 1, 51-57.

Lovegrove, W. (1994). Visual deficit in dyslexia: evidence and implications. In A. Fawcett & R. Nicolson (Eds.) *Dyslexia in Children.* Hemel Hempstead, Herts: Harvester Wheatsheaf.

Lyytinen (1997). In search of the precursors of dyslexia: A prospective study of children at risk of reading problems. In C. Hulme & M. Snowling (Eds.) *Dyslexia: Biology, Cognition and Intervention.* London: Whurr.

MacKay, T. (1999). Education and the disadvantaged: Is there any justice. *The Psychologist, 12,* 7, 344-349.

McNab, I. (1994). Specific learning difficulties: how severe is severe? *BAS information booklet.* Windsor: NFER-Nelson.

Manis, F.R., Seidenberg, M.S., Doi, L.M., McBride-Chang, C. & Petersen, A. (1996). On the bases of two subtypes of developmental dyslexia. *Cognition, 58,* 157-195.

Mann, V.A. (1986). Why some children encounter reading problems: The contribution of difficulties with language processing and phonological sophistication to early reading disability. In Torgenson, J.K. & Wong, B.Y.L. (Eds.) *Psychological and educational perspectives on learning disabilities.* New York: Academic Press.

Marsh, H.W. (1992). Content specificity of relations between academic achievement and academic self-concept. *Journal of Educational Psychology, 84,* 1, 35-42.

Masutto, C., Bravar, L. & Fabbro, F. (1994). Neurolinguistic differentiation of children with subtypes of dyslexia. *Journal of Learning Disabilities, 27,* 8, 520-526.

Maughan, B. (1994). Behavioural development and reading disability. In C. Hulme & M Snowling (Eds.) *Reading Development and Dyslexia.* London: Whurr.

McGee, R., Share, D., Moffitt, T.E., Williams, S. & Silva, P.A. (1988). Reading disability, behaviour problems and juvenile delinquency. In D.H. Saklofske & S.B.G. Eysenck (Eds.) *Individual Differences in Children and Adolescents.* London: Hodder & Stoughton.

Melikian, B.A. (1990). Family characteristics of children with dyslexia. *Journal of Learning Disabilities, 23,* 386-391.

Miles, E. (1995). Can there be a single definition of dyslexia? *Dyslexia, 1,* 37-45.

Miles, T.R. (1983). *Dyslexia: The Pattern of Difficulties (First Edition).* London: Harvester Wheatsheaf.

Miles, T.R. (1993). *Dyslexia: The Pattern of Difficulties (Second Edition).* London: Whurr.

Miles, T.R. (1996). Do dyslexic children have IQs? *Dyslexia, 2,* 3, 175-178.

Miles, T.R. & Miles, E. (1999). *Dyslexia: 100 years on. (Second Edition).* Milton Keynes: Open University Press.

Millard, E. (1997). *Differently Literate: Boys, Girls and the Schooling of Literacy.* London: Falmer Press.

Morris, R.D., Steubing, K.K., Fletcher, J.M., Shaywitz, S.E., Lyon, G.R. Shankweiler, D.P.,

Katz, L., Francis, D.J. & Shaywitz, B.A. (1998). Subtypes of reading disability: Variability around a phonological core. *Journal of Educational Psychology, 90, 3,* 347-373.

Morton, J. & Frith, U. (1995). Causal modelling: A structural approach to developmental psychopathology. In D. Cicchetti & D.J. Cohen (Eds.) *Manual of Developmental Psychopathology* (pp.357-390). NY Psychological Assessment of Dyslexia: Wiley.

Morton, L.L. (1994). Interhemispheric balance patterns detected by selective phonemic dichotic laterality measures in four clinical subtypes of reading disabled children. *Journal of Clinical and Experimental Neuropsychology, 16, 4,* 556-567.

Neuman, S.B. & McCormick, S. (Eds.) (1995). *Single Subject Experimental Research: Applications for Literacy.* Newark, Delaware: International Reading Association.

Nicolson, R.I. & Fawcett, A.J. (1990). Automaticity: A New Framework for Dyslexia Research. *Cognition, 35,* 159-182.

Nicolson, R.I. & Fawcett, A.J. (1995). Dyslexia is more than a phonological disability. Dyslexia: *An International Journal of Research and Practice, 1,* 19-37.

Oakhill, J., Cain, K. & Yuill, N. (1998). Individual differences in children's comprehension skill: Toward an integrated model. In C. Hulme & R. M. Joshi (Eds.) *Reading and Spelling: Development and Disorders.* London: Lawrence Erlbaum.

Osmond, J. (1993). *The Reality of Dyslexia.* London: Cassell.

Paulesu, E., Frith, U., Snowling, M., Gallagher, A., Morton, J., Frackowiak, R.S.J., & Frith, C.D. (1996). Is developmental dyslexia a disconnection syndrome? Evidence from PET scanning. *Brain, 119,* 143-157.

Pennington, B.F. (1990). The genetics of dyslexia. *Journal of Child Psychology and Psychiatry, 31,* 193-201.

Perfetti, C.A., Rieben, L. & Fayol, M. (Eds.) (1997). *Learning to Spell: Research, Theory and Practice across Languages.* London: Lawrence Erlbaum.

Perfetti, C.A. & Zhang, S.L. (1995). Very early phonological activation in Chinese reading. *Cognition, 21,* 24-33.

Pianta, R.C. & Caldwell, C.B. (1990). Stability of externalising symptoms from kindergarten to first grade and factors related to instability. *Development and Psychopathology, 2,* 247-258.

Pietrowski, J. & Reason, R. (in press). The National Literacy Strategy and Dyslexia: A comparison of teaching methods and materials. *Support for Learning, 15,* 1.

Pitt, M.A. & Samuel, A.G. (1995). Lexical and Sublexical Feedback in Auditory Word Recognition. *Cognitive Psychology 29,* 149-188.

Plaut, D.C., McClelland, J.L., Seidenberg, M.S. & Patterson, K. (1996). Understanding normal and impaired word reading: Computational principles in quasi-regular domains. *Psychological Review, 103, 1,* 56-115.

Plunkett, K., Karmiloff-Smith, A., Bates, E., Elman, J.L. & Johnson, M.H. (1997). Connectionism and developmental psychology. *Journal of Child Psychology and Psychiatry, 38, 1,* 53-80.

Pollatsek, A., Lesch, M., Morris, R.K. & Rayner, K. (1992). Phonological Codes are used in Integrating Information across Saccades in Word Identification and Reading. *Journal of Experimental Psychology: Human Perception and Performance, 18, 1,* 148-162.

Pumfrey, P.D. (1996). *Specific Developmental Dyslexia: Basics to Back?* Leicester: The Education Section of The British Psychological Society.

Pumfrey, P.D. (1997). Assessment of affective and motivational aspects of reading. In J.R. Beech & C. Singleton (Eds.) *The Psychological Assessment of Reading.* London: Routledge.

Pumfrey, P. & Reason, R. (1991). *Specific Learning Difficulties (Dyslexia): Challenges and Responses.* London: Routledge.

Rack, J.P. (1994). Dyslexia: The phonological deficit hypothesis. In Fawcett, A., & Nicolson, R. (Eds.) *Dyslexia in children: Multi-disciplinary perspectives.* London: Harvester Wheatsheaf.

Rack, J., Hulme, C. & Snowling, M. (1993). Learning to read: a theoretical synthesis. In H. Reece (Ed.) *Advances in Child Development and Behaviour, Vol. 24* (pp.99-132). New York: Academic Press.

Rack, J.P., Snowling, M. & Olson, R.K. (1992). The non-word reading deficit in developmental dyslexia. *Reading Research Quarterly, 27,* 1, 29-53.

Raybould, E.C. & Solity, J. (1982). Teaching with precision. *Special Education Forward Trends, 8,* 2, 9-13.

Rayner, K. & Morris, R.K. (1992). Eye Movement Control in Reading: Evidence against Semantic Preprocessing. *J. Exp. Psychology: Human Perception and Performance, 18,* 1, 163-172.

Reason, R. (1998a). Does the 'specific' in specific learning difficulties now make a difference to the way we teach? *Educational and Child Psychology, 15,* 1, 71-83.

Reason, R. (1998b) How relevant is connectioninst modelling of reading to educational practice? *Educational and Child Psychology, 15,* 2, 59-65.

Rego, L.B. & Bryant, P.E. (1993). The connection between phonological, syntactic and semantic skills and children's reading and spelling. *European Journal of Psychology of Education, 8,* 3, 235-246.

Richards, S.B., Taylor, R.L., Ramasamy, R. & Richards, R.Y. (1999). *Single Subject Research: Applications in Educational and Clinical Settings*. San Diego: Singular Publishing Group.

Riddick, B. (1996). *Living with Dyslexia.* London: Routledge.

Rourke, B.P. (1988). Socio-emotional disturbances in learning disabled children. *Journal of Consulting and Clinical Psychology, 56,* 6, 801-810.

Roth, F.R.P. Speece, D.R., Cooper, D.H. & Dulapaz, S. (1996). Unresolved Mysteries: How do Metalinguistic and Narrative Skills Connect with Early Reading? Journal of Special Education, 30, 3, 257-277.

Rubin, D. (1997). *Diagnosis and Correction in Reading Instruction (Third Edition).* New York: Allun & Bacon.

Rutter, M. (1998). Dyslexia: Approaches to validation. *Child Psychology and Psychiatry Review, 3,* 1, 24-25.

Scarborough, H.S. (1990). Very early language deficits in dyslexic children. *Child Development, 61,* 1728-1743.

Scarborough, H.S. (1991). Early syntactic development of dyslexic children. *Annals of Dyslexia, 44,* 207-220.

Seidenberg, M.S., Bruck, M., Fornarolo, G. & Backman, J. (1985). Word recognition processes of poor and disabled readers: do they necessarily differ? *Applied Psycholinguistics, 6,* 161-180.

Seidenberg, M. & McClelland, J. (1989). A distributed, developmental model of word recognition and naming. *Psychological Review, 96,* 523-568.

Seymour, P.H.K. (1998). Beyond the phonological deficit hypothesis. *Child Psychology and Psychiatry Review, 3,* 1, 22-23.

Seymour, P.H.K. & Evans, H.M. (1994). Levels of phonological awareness and learning to read. *Reading and Writing, 6,* 221-250.

Shankweiler D. & Crain S. (1986). Language mechanisms and reading disorder: A modular approach. *Cognition, 24,* 139-64.

Share, D.L. (1995). Phonological Recoding and Self-teaching: Sine qua non of Reading Acquisition. *Cognition, 55,* 151-218.

Share, D.L. (1996). Word recognition and spelling processes in specific reading disabled and garden-variety poor readers. *Dyslexia, 2,* 3, 167-174.

Share, D.L., McGee, R., McKenzie, D., Williams, A. & Silva, P.A. (1987). Further evidence relating to the distinction between specific reading retardation and general reading backwardness. *British Journal of Developmental Psychology, 5,* 35-44.

Share, D.L. & Stanovich, K.E. (1995). Cognitive Processes in Early Reading Development: Accommodating Individual Differences into a Model of Acquisition. *Issues in Education, 1,* 1, 1-57.

Siegel, L.S. (1988.) Evidence that IQ scores are irrelevant to the definition and analysis of reading disability. *Canadian Journal of Psychology, 42,* 201-215.

Siegel, L. S. (1989). IQ is irrelevant to the definition of learning disabilities. *Journal of Learning Disabilities, 22,* 469-478.

Siegel, L.S. (1992). An evaluation of the discrepancy definition of dyslexia. *Journal of Learning Disabilities, 25,* 618-629.

Siegel, L.S., Share, D. & Geva, E. (1995). Evidence for Superior Orthographic Skills in Dyslexics. *Psychological Science, 6,* 4, 250-254.

Singleton, C. (1998). *Dyslexia in Higher Education: Policy, Provision and Practice.* Hull: The University of Hull.

Smith, F. (Ed.) (1973). *Psycholinguistics and Reading.* New York: Holt, Rinehart & Winston.

Snowling, M.J. (1987). *Dyslexia: A Cognitive-Developmental Perspective.* Oxford: Blackwell.

Snowling, M.J. (1991). Developmental reading disorders. *Journal of Child Psychology and Psychiatry, 32,* 49-77.

Snowling, M.J. (1995). Phonological processing and developmental dyslexia. *Journal of Research in Reading, 18,* 132-138.

Snowling, M.J. (1998a). Dyslexia as a phonological deficit: Evidence and implications. *Child Psychology and Psychiatry Review, 3,* 1, 4-11.

Snowling, M.J. (1998b). Reading development and its difficulties. *Educational and Child Psychology 15,* 2, 44-58.

Snowling, M.J. & Nation, K. (1997). Development and dyslexia : Further comments on Ellis, McDougall & Monk. *Dyslexia, 3,* 9-11.

Snowling, M.J. & Stackhouse, J. (Eds.) (1996). *Dyslexia, Speech, and Language.* London: Whurr.

Solity, J. (1991). Special needs – a discriminatory concept? *Educational Psychology in Practice, 7,* 1, 12-19.

Solity, J. (1996). Discrepancy definitions of dyslexia: An assessment through teaching perspective. *Educational Psychology in Practice, 12,* 3, 141-151.

Solity, J. & Bull, S. (1987). *Special Needs: Bridging the Curriculum Gap.* Milton Keynes: OU Press.

Spafford, C.S., & Grosser, G.S. (1993). The social misperception syndrome in children with learning disabilities: Social causes versus neurological variables. *Journal of Learning Disabilities, 26,* 3, 178-189.

Spafford, S. (1989). Wechsler digit span subtest: diagnostic usefulness with dyslexic children. *Perceptual and Motor Skills, 69,* 115-125.

Speece, D.L., McKinney, J.D. & Appelbaum, M.I. (1985). Classification and validation of behavioural subtypes of learning-disabled children. *Journal of Educational Psychology, 77,* 67-77.

Stackhouse, J. & Wells, B. (1997). How do speech and language problems affect literacy development? In C. Hulme & M. Snowling (Eds.) *Dyslexia: Biology, Cognition and Intervention.* London: Whurr.

Stanovich, K.E. (1986). Cognitive processes and reading problems of learning-disabled children: Evaluation and assumption of specificity. In J.K. Torgesen & B. Wong (Eds.) *Psychological and Educational Perspectives on Learning Disabilities.* New York: Academic Press.

Stanovich, K.E. (1991). Discrepancy definitions of reading disability: Has intelligence led us astray? *Reading Research Quarterly, 26,* 1, 7-29.

Stanovich, K.E. (1996). Towards a more inclusive definition of dyslexia. *Dyslexia, 2,* 3, 154-166.

Stanovich, K.E. (1998). Refining the phonological core deficit model. *Child Psychology and Psychiatry Review, 3,* 1, 17-21.

Stanovich, K.E., Siegel, L.S. & Gottardo, A. (1997a). Progress in the search for dyslexia subtypes. In C. Hulme & M. Snowling (Eds.) *Dyslexia: Biology, Cognition and Intervention.* London: Whurr.

Stanovich, K.E., Siegel, L.S. & Gottardo, A. (1997b). Converging evidence for phonological and surface subtypes of reading disability. *Journal of Educational Psychology, 89,* 114-127.

Stanovich, K.E., Siegel, L.S., Gottardo, A., Chiappe, P. & Sidhu, R. (1997c). Subtypes of developmental dyslexia: Differences in phonological coding and orthographic coding. In B. Blachman (Ed.) *Foundations of Reading Acquisition and Dyslexia.* London: Lawrence Erlbaum.

Stanovich, K.E. & Stanovich, P.J. (1997). Further thoughts on aptitude/achievement discrepancy. *Educational Psychology in Practice, 13,* 1, 3-8.

Stein, J.F. (1994). A visual defect in dyslexics? In A. Fawcett & R. Nicolson (Eds.) *Dyslexia in Children.* Hemel Hempstead, Herts: Harvester Wheatsheaf.

Stein, J. & Monaco, T. (1998). Cited in *Times Educational Supplement* 27.02.1998.

Stein, J., Richardson, A. & Fowler, S. (1998). Letter to the editor re a comparison of dyslexic and normal readers using orthoptic assessment procedures. *Dyslexia, 4,* 109-110.

Stothard, S.E., Snowling, M.J., Bishop, D.V.M., Chipchase, B.B. & Kaplan, C.A. (1998). Language impaired pre-schoolers: A follow-up into adolescence. *Journal of Speech, Language and Hearing Research, 41,* 407-418.

Street, B. (1995). *Social Literacies: Critical Approaches to Literacy in Development, Ethnography and Education.* London: Longman.

Tallal, P., Miller, S.L., Jenkins, W.M. & Merzenich, M.M. (1997). The role of temporal processing in developmental language-based disorders: Research and clinical implications. In B.A. Blachman (Ed.) *Foundations of Reading Acquisition and Dyslexia: Implications for Early Intervention*. Mahwah, NJ, USA: Lawrence Erlbaum Associates.

Tan, L.H., Hoosain, R., & Siok, W.W.T. (1996). Activation of Phonological Codes Before Access to Character Meaning in Written Chinese. *Journal of Experimental Psychology: Learning, Memory and Cognition 22*, 4, 865-882.

Thomson, M.E. (1989). *Developmental Dyslexia (Third Edition)*. London : Whurr.

Thousand, J.S. & Villa, R.A. (1991). Accommodating for greater student variance. In M. Ainscow (Ed.) *Effective Schools for All*. London: David Fulton.

Tonnessen, F.E. (1997). How can we best define dyslexia? *Dyslexia, 3*, 78-92.

Torgensen, H. (1986). Controlling for IQ. *Journal of Learning Disabilities, 19*, 452-460.

Treiman, R. (1998). Spelling in normal children and dyslexics. In B.A. Blachman (Ed.) *Foundations of Reading Acquisition and Dyslexia*. London: Lawrence Erlbaum.

Treiman, R. & Zukowski, A. (1991). Levels of phonological awareness. In S. Brady & D. Shankweiler (Eds.) *Phonological Processing in Literacy*. London: Lawrence Erlbaum.

Tunmer, W.E. & Chapman, J.W. (1996). A developmental model of dyslexia: Can the construct be saved? *Dyslexia, 2*, 3, 179-189.

Turner, M. (1997). *Psychological Assessment of Dyslexia*. London: Whurr.

Tyler, S. (1990). Subtypes of specific learning difficulties: a review. In P.D. Pumfrey & C.D. Elliott (Eds.) *Children's Difficulties in Reading, Spelling and Writing*. Basingstoke, Hants: Falmer Press.

Van de Stoel, S. (1990). *Parents on Dyslexia*. Avon: Multilingual Matters.

Van Den Bos, K.P. (1996). Review on the balance model of dyslexia. *Dyslexia, 2*, 212-213.

Van Orden, G. (1991). Phonological mediation is fundamental to word reading. In D. Besner & G.W. Humphries (Eds.) *Basic Processes in Reading: Visual Word Recognition*. London: Lawrence Erlbaum.

Van Strien, J.W., Stolk, B.D. & Zuiker, S. (1995). Hemisphere-specific treatment of dyslexia subtypes: Better reading with anxiety- laden words. *Journal of Learning Disabilities, 28*, 1, 30-34.

Vellutino, F.R., Scanlon, D., Sipay, E.R., Small, S.G., Pratt, A., Cohen, R. & Denckla, M.B. (1996). Cognitive profiles of difficult-to-remediate and readily remediated poor readers: Early intervention as a vehicle for distinguishing between cognitive and experiential deficits as basic causes of specific reading disability. *Journal of Educational Psychology, 88*, 4, 601-638.

Wallace, C. (1986). *Learning to Read in a Multicultural Society: The Social Context of Second Language Literacy*. Oxford: Pergamon.

Wang, M.C. (1991). Adaptive instruction: An alternative approach to providing for student diversity. In M. Ainscow (Ed.) *Effective Schools for All*. London: David Fulton.

Wasik, B.A. & Slavin, R.E. (1994). Preventing reading failure with one-to-one tutoring: A review of five programmes. *Reading Research Quarterly, 28*, 178-200.

Watson, C. & Willows, D.M. (1993). Evidence for a visual-processing-deficit subtype among disabled readers. In D.M. Willows, R.S. Kruk & E. Corcos (Eds.) *Visual Processes in Reading Disabilities*. Hillsdale NJ: Lawrence Erlbaum.

Wechsler, D. (1992). *The Wechsler Intelligence Scale for Children – Third Edition (WISC-III).* New York: The Psychological Corporation.

Weiner, B. (1995). A cognitive-emotional-action sequence: anticipated emotional consequences of causal attributions and reported communication strategy. *Developmental Psychology, 21,* 1, 102-107.

Wilkins, A. (1993). Reading and visual discomfort. In D.M. Willows, R.S. Kruk & E. Corcos (Eds.) *Visual Processes in Reading Disabilities.* Hillsdale NJ: Lawrence Erlbaum.

Williams, H. & Muncey, J. (1982). Precision teaching before behavioural objectives. *Journal of the Association of Educational Psychologists, 5,* 8, 40-42.

Willows, D.M., Kruk, R.S. & Corcos, E. (1993). Are there differences between disabled and normal readers in their processing of visual information? In D.M. Willows, R.S. Kruk & E. Corcos (Eds.) *Visual Processes in Reading Disabilities.* Hillsdale NJ: Lawrence Erlbaum.

Willows, D.M., Kruk, R.S. & Corcos, E. (Eds.) (1993). *Visual Processes in Reading Disabilities.* Hillsdale NJ: Lawrence Erlbaum.

Wolfendale, S. (1993). Thirty years of change: Children with special educational needs. *Children and Society, 7,* 1, 82-94.

Woods, K. (1998). Consideration of dyslexia through different psychological paradigms. *Educational Psychology in Practice, 13,* 4, 274-278.

Woods, K. & Reason, R. (1999) Concentrating in exams. *Educational Psychology in Practice, 15,* 1.

Woods, K. & Reason, R. (in press). The provision of prompters and supervised breaks during GCSE examinations. *Educational Psychology in Practice.*

Yasutake, D. & Bryan, T. (1995). The influence of affect on the achievement and behaviour of students with learning disabilities. *Journal of Learning Disabilities, 28,* 6, 329-334.

Yesseldyke, J.E. & Christenson, S.L. (1987). Evaluating students' instructional environments. *Remedial and Special Education, 8,* 3, 17-24.

Zatz, S. & Chassin, L. (1985). Cognitions of test-anxious children under naturalistic test-taking conditions. *Journal of Consulting and Clinical Psychology, 53,* 3, 393-401

ACKNOWLEDGEMENTS

The Working Party would like to acknowledge with gratitude all the responses received to the draft report circulated for consultation in January 1999. Appendix B provides an analysis of the views and suggestions of the respondents. As responses on behalf of working groups or educational psychology services did not usually state all the names of the educational psychologists involved in the consultation, we list below the Local Education Authority Psychological Services in the UK from which individual or collective responses were received. We are also grateful to respondents working in other contexts whose names are too numerous to be listed here.

LEAS IN ENGLAND

Barnsley
Bedfordshire
Birmingham (Central and North)
Birmingham (South)
Blackburn and Darwen
Bracknell Forest
Bradford
Bristol
Buckinghamshire
Cumbria
Derbyshire
Devon
Dorset
Dudley
East Sussex
Essex
Gateshead
Gloucestershire
Hampshire
Kent
Kirklees
Knowsley
Lancashire
Leeds
Leicester City
Leicestershire
Manchester
Medway
Milton Keynes
Newcastle upon Tyne
Norfolk
North Lincolnshire

North Somerset
North Yorkshire
Nottinghamshire County
Oldham
Oxfordshire
Portsmouth
Rochdale
Rutland
Salford
Sheffield
Somerset
South Gloucestershire
Staffordshire
Suffolk
Surrey
Telford and Wrekin
Torbay
Wakefield
Walsall
Warrington
Warwickshire
West Sussex
Windsor and Maidenhead
Worcestershire

London Boroughs
Barking and Dagenham
Bexley
Bromley
Ealing
Enfield
Greenwich

Haringey
Harrow
Havering
Hillingdon
Kensington and Chelsea
Lewisham
Newham
Richmond upon Thames
Southwark
Sunderland
Tower Hamlets
Westminster

LEAs in Wales
Isle of Anglesey
Blaenau Gwent
Cardiff
Flintshire
Monmouthshire
Neath Port Talbot
Powys
Wrexham

LEAs in Northern Ireland
Belfast Education and Library Board
NE Education and Library Board
SE Education and Library Board
W Education and Library Board

Other organisations represented by the responses
Association of Educational Psychologists
The British Dyslexia Association
The British Psychological Society Scottish
    Division of Educational Psychology
The British Psychological Society Special
    Group in Clinical Neuropsychology
    (DCP)
Helen Arkell Dyslexia Centre

Assistance by academic researchers
We are particularly grateful for the suggestions and assistance provided by the following cognitive researchers with expertise in the field of literacy learning and/or literacy difficulties.

Dr. Lynne Duncan,
University of Dundee
Professor Uta Frith,
Institute of Cognitive Neuroscience, UCL
Dr. Nata Goulandris,
University College London
Professor Usha Goswami,
Institute of Child Health, UCL
Professor Tim and Mrs Elaine Miles,
University of Wales, Bangor
Professor John Morton,
Institute of Cognitive Nuroscience, UCL
Professor Peter Pumfrey,
University of Manchester
Dr. Gavin Reid,
University of Edinburgh
Professor Philip Seymour,
University of Dundee
Dr. David Share,
University of Haifa

Appendix A:
EDUCATIONAL PSYCHOLOGY SERVICE POLICIES AND PRACTICES
Summary of Responses to the DECP Working Party Survey – March 1998

INTRODUCTION

In order to gain a picture of current policies and practices, a questionnaire was circulated to local authority educational psychology services in March 1998. The questionnaire requested documentary evidence where available and covered issues of service/local authority policy, factors influencing policy, provision made, criteria for access to provision and the particular issues that respondents would wish the DECP Working Party to consider. Information was received from 60 educational psychology services (representing about 40 per cent of services in England and Wales). Results are presented in summary form below. The responses are not necessarily representative of practices in all services but provide an indication of current trends.

QUESTION 1

(a) Does your service/LEA have an assessment policy on dyslexia/SpLD?
   If yes, are you prepared to provide the working party with a copy?

(b) If you do identify this particular difficulty, what is it called?

(a) Assessment policies and documents

Interpretation of 'assessment policy' on dyslexia/specific learning difficulties varied widely and respondents recording the existence of policies referred to, or supplied, documentation which included: Local education authority general policies on identification, assessment and provision to meet special educational needs; extracts from local authority policies on special educational needs with particular reference to dyslexia/specific learning difficulties; local authority policy statements on specific learning difficulties or dyslexia; descriptions of criteria for triggering Code of Practice Stage 4 statutory assessment in response to learning difficulties/dyslexia; descriptions of criteria for accessing local authority Stage 5 provision for specific learning difficulties; 'position statements' on specific learning difficulties/dyslexia; local authority guides to specific learning difficulties; specific learning difficulty/dyslexia guidelines for good practice (including assessment practice); general assessment policies for educational psychologists; general assessment policies for educational psychologists and teachers; and one document headed 'Psychological Assessment of Specific Learning Difficulties'.

This range of 'policy' was reported by 26 (43 per cent) respondents. There were an additional 9 (15 per cent) references to, or attachments, which would fit into this broad classification. Of further note, 44 (73 per cent) respondents recorded later that their LEAs use criteria for decisions regarding access to local authority specific learning difficulties provision, most of whom could provide these in written form. On the basis of the range of responses described above, it would seem safe to conclude that at least 75 per cent of respondent services/local authorities have policy documentation of some description and several others are working on policy development.

Much of the documentation provided, or referred to, appears to reflect an emphasis on criteria for access to Stage 4 assessment or Stage 5 provision. Where assessment was described, it referred extensively to the staged process advised in the Code of Practice on the Identification and Assessment of Special Educational Needs (DfEE, 1994). The sections relating to specific learning difficulties in particular (Sections 3.60–3.63) were quoted in the body of educational psychology service/local authority literature.

(b) Labelling the difficulty

30 (50 per cent) respondent services referred to this learning difficulty as a 'specific learning difficulty'; 22 (37 per cent) use both 'dyslexia' and 'specific learning difficulty'; 1 uses 'dyslexia; 7 (4 per cent) services recorded alternatives: 'specific learning difficulties/dyslexia' (2), 'specific learning difficulties (dyslexia)' (3), 'Specific literacy difficulty' (1), 'whatever parents feel most comfortable with' (1). Some respondents added that their services were not too concerned about the terminology adopted. It may be concluded from this data that the term 'dyslexia' is now more widely accepted than some nine years ago when the previous DECP survey was carried out (see Section 2.2 in the main report).

QUESTION 2

What factors informed/influenced the drawing up of this policy?

30 (50 per cent) respondents provided information about the factors that had informed/influenced policy. 15 (25 per cent) cited factors relating to the need for ensuring consistent, 'defensible' approaches to assessment and to decision-making about access to additional resources. Other factors cited were as follows:

✦ Developments in research and practice.

✦ The need to ensure quality of practice.

✦ The view that school-based assessment and National Curriculum teacher assessment should pre-date educational psychology assessment/involvement.

✦ Belief that assessment should be conducted over time and be informed by pupils' responses to intervention.

✦ Recognition that SpLD are represented at all stages of the Code of Practice.

✦ The need to improve awareness and services to children with literacy problems.

✦ Recognition that early identification and intervention are necessary to prevent the possibility of later development of behaviour difficulties.

✦ Desire to see educational psychologists actively involved in supporting schools to meet needs prior to the Code of Practice Stage 3.

✦ The need to utilise the skills and experience of teachers qualified in teaching pupils experiencing SpLD.

+ Belief in partnership in assessment which should include pupils, parents, teachers and educational psychologists.

+ Recognition that parents need reassurance that needs of their children are being met.

Overall, respondents' comments indicated:

+ A wish to set specific learning difficulties in the wider context of literacy development and the related range of difficulties rather than to separate it and give it elevated or different status and 'treatment'. Most LEAs reflect this principle in practice, particularly at Stage 3, but the majority have criteria and make provision for SpLD at Stage 5, as will be seen in responses to the next question.

+ Assessment of and intervention in relation to SpLD are largely seen to be the responsibilities of mainstream schools with educational psychologists, ideally, supporting schools in identifying and meeting needs.

+ Much concern is expressed, however, about the effects of legal action upon educational psychology assessment practice reported to be in danger of becoming increasingly defensive. Colleagues feel pressure to adopt practices not supported by research evidence. Some responses express particular unease about use of the discrepancy model which some LEAs/educational psychology services have adopted to provide visible consistency and accountability in their decision-making about access to additional resources for specific learning difficulties. The practice of allocating these resources only to pupils within particular ability ranges raises questions of equal opportunity for many respondents and definitive guidance on this matter is sought.

QUESTION 3

(a) Does the LEA make provision for pupils with dyslexia/specific learning difficulties?

(b) Please describe this provision.

46 (77 per cent) respondents recorded that provision is made at Stage 3; 10 (17 per cent) respondents recorded that provision is not made at this stage. 58 (97 per cent) respondents recorded that provision is made at Stage 5; 1 respondent recorded that provision is not made at this stage.

The following range of Stage 3 provision was described:

+ Guidelines to schools on recognising and teaching pupils with dyslexia/SpLD.

+ Needs to be met from within the mainstream school's own resources supported by the delegated special educational needs budget.

+ General learning support teacher advice for example on IEP.

+ Specialist learning support teacher advice.

+ Assessment by EP with input to IEP with SENCO.

+ Training for mainstream staff (some to RSA SpLD Diploma).

+ Sessional direct teaching from outreach learning support teacher in mainstream school.

+ Sessional direct teaching from outreach specialist support teacher in mainstream school.

- Attendance at Reading Centre.
- Off-site tutorial support.
- Attendance at unit in mainstream school.
- Attendance at resourced mainstream school.
- A combination of some of the above provisions.

The following range of Stage 5 provision was described:
(It can be noted that most are also available at Stage 3.)

- A combination of some of the provisions at Stage 3.
- Further delegated funding for school to buy in additional support.
- Additional training for classroom assistants via distance learning packages.
- Enhanced learning support in school either by outreach teacher or learning support assistant.
- Sessional direct teaching from outreach specialist learning support teacher in mainstream school.
- Attendance at resourced mainstream provisions, particularly at secondary school level.
- Out-county placements in special units, resourced schools and, exceptionally, specialist day and residential schools.

QUESTION 4

(a) Is access to provision governed by specific criteria?

(b) If yes, are you prepared to provide a copy? (Please attach)

44 (73 per cent) respondents reported that access to assessment and provision at Stage 3 and/or Stage 4 and/or Stage 5 is governed by criteria. 25 (42 per cent) provided copies of documentation which described these criteria.

The practices of local education authorities, educational psychology services and learning support services are set within the staged process advised in the Code of Practice on Special Educational Needs (DfEE, 1994). Guidance in the Code of Practice (Sections 3.60–3.63) on identification, assessment and provision to meet specific learning difficulties is reflected directly in many responses and shapes the assessment process, content and decision-making in most authorities.

Before there can be consideration of Stage 4 assessment, it is expected that schools will have taken regard to the Code of Practice and will be able to provide well documented evidence of 'relevant and purposeful intervention' over time at Stage 2 from 'within their own resources' and in collaboration with the LEA and its services at Stage 3. Some documentation states that 'over time' at each stage should be at least six months and should include two recorded reviews. Evidence from the beginning of Stage 2 is reported to require clear targets, modes of assessment, outcomes and individual educational plans revised as a result of reviews. One respondent's guidance advises that the SMART characteristics of a good target should be observed i.e. **S**pecific, **M**easurable, **A**chievable, **R**ealistic (in terms of expectations of the child) and **T**imescaled.

National Curriculum attainments are reported, either explicitly or implicitly, to be a (or the) principal measure of a pupil's progress, and access to the curriculum is a (or the) central issue in considering children's special educational needs.

Guidance for the delivery of the National Curriculum is cited by one respondent as being sufficiently flexible to accommodate the minority of pupils with learning difficulties who may need to be taught at Level 1 in some subjects at their Key Stage, or who may need to follow programmes of study related to an earlier Key Stage, thus reducing the need for disapplication or modification of the curriculum requiring a Statement of Special Educational Need.

On the whole, significantly low levels of performance, particularly in core literacy and numeracy areas of the curriculum, would be required to suggest learning difficulties which are serious enough to raise the question of a statutory Stage 4 assessment. The number of children functioning at this level and requiring provision to be specified in a Statement is estimated generally to be 2 per cent or fewer of the child population. Those children considered to be experiencing severe specific learning difficulties are reported to make up a small number within this overall figure.

It is particularly important to note that respondents' working criteria vary according to the overall special educational needs policies, practices and patterns of provision and support in their particular local education authorities. The combinations of criteria adopted, therefore, are meaningful only in their particular contexts. These combinations of criteria are drawn from the following categories of information:

✦ Records of progress and action at Stages 1–3.

✦ National Curriculum attainment levels.

✦ Extreme discrepancies between attainments in different core subjects of the National Curriculum or within one subject e.g. English.

✦ Results from standardised tests of reading, spelling, writing and mathematics attainments.

✦ Discrepancies between actual scores on appropriate attainment tests and those expected on the basis of performance on tests of cognitive ability.

✦ Recorded evidence of associated difficulties in attention, working memory, sequencing and motor coordination.

✦ Recorded evidence of associated emotional and behavioural difficulties.

✦ Evidence that literacy problems are not primarily explained by:

  – significant delay or disorder in linguistic development;

  – significant sensory or physical impairment;

  – significant neurological impairment;

  – significant environmental, cultural or economic factors;

  – poor school attendance or lack of educational opportunity;

  – significant and unrelated emotional and behavioural difficulties.

QUESTION 5

Summarise below any particular issues you would wish the DECP Working Party to be aware of and to consider.

A wide range of issues, concerns and proposals was brought to the Working Party's attention. This range is reflected in the following sub-categories and illustrative extracts from responses.

Concepts/definitions/models of specific learning difficulties (dyslexia)

Should we move towards a model which includes all children and young people with literacy difficulties?

We need to 'do away with' SpLD as a separate category. We need to view pupils as having learning difficulties and then pursue a 'needs led' problem solving approach.

Does diagnosis of SpLD indicate at least average general ability?

SpLD is only one part of literacy difficulty and all SEN in general.

Please advise on the place of SpLD on the continuum of learning difficulties.

Would the working party establish clear definitions of the different forms of SpLD and also identify how language deficits may affect learning and yet not be held to be SpLD.

Please advise on the validity of the term 'dyslexia'.

Assessment in the context of intervention

Diagnosis is less important than intervention.

It would be helpful to have advice on properly researched effective teaching approaches and alternative provisions.

What works? What effect does a personal computer have?

How effective are multi-sensory methods?

Do we know that slow children need to be taught to read in a different way to generally able children with literacy difficulties?

We need to link intervention to the National Literacy Strategy.

Approaches to assessment and models of assessment

We need to be clear about the purpose of assessment. The purpose of psychological assessment is to bring about change via identification of need and planning of appropriate intervention programmes – in the context of educational provision.

What is distinctive about EP assessment as opposed to specialist teacher assessment?

An interactive model of assessment should be emphasised as opposed to the limitations of clinic based non-contextualised assessment.

We should move towards a more functional/problem solving/empirical assessment through teaching model which takes account of the child's educational environment.

It would be helpful to have an assessment model which can be used by teachers in consultation with EPs.

We should emphasise the importance of 'early ' assessment preferably on a Reading Recovery model for all children who might conceivably need it.

It would be helpful to have advice about the range of assessment approaches it would be valid for an EP to use.

Advice on culture-fair assessment techniques would be helpful.

A statement should be made that where psychometric measures are used they must be valid, reliable, up to date and reported in full.

Please address the relevance of the ability/attainment discrepancy model.

The relationship between the concepts of specific learning difficulties/dyslexia and special educational needs

Advice on the criteria against which to measure requests for Stage 4 assessment/Stage 5 provision would be welcome.

Why should more able children with dyslexia get preferential access to resources compared to other pupils with learning difficulties and less able children with dyslexia?

There is great difficulty in devising criteria that are justifiable in terms of assessment and at the same time easily understood and transparent to teachers and parents.

We need advice on appropriate practice to avoid the charge of not fulfilling the duty of care.

What would constitute a reasonable assessment?

Specific learning difficulties need to be viewed in relation to other serious difficulties and the danger of imbalance in the allocation of resources monitored and addressed.

The need for a consistent approach that has sufficient flexibility to incorporate all valid paradigms of psychological assessment

We need a consistent approach to identification and assessment.

The worst possible outcome from this exercise would be to define a process which we would need to follow slavishly or risk being taken to court.

CONCLUSION

Bearing in mind that the survey is not necessarily representative of practices in all services, the following trends may be discerned from the data:

✦ At least 75 per cent of respondent services/local authorities appear to have policy documentation that is relevant for specific learning difficulties/dyslexia and several others are working on policy development.

- It may be concluded from our data that the term 'dyslexia' is now more widely accepted than some nine years ago when the previous DECP survey was carried out (Pumfrey & Reason, 1991)

- Respondents emphasise the need to ensure a consistent approach to assessment and to decision making about access to additional resources. Current practice follows closely the staged process of the framework provided by the Code of Practice (DfEE, 1994).

- There is considerable similarity between the range of provision made at stages 3 and 5 of the Code of Practice.

- There is a strong wish to set specific learning difficulties/dyslexia in the wider context of literacy learning and development.

- Assessment of and intervention in relation to dyslexia/specific learning difficulties is seen largely to be the responsibility of mainstream schools with educational psychologists supporting schools in identifying and meeting needs.

- Resource criteria vary according to overall special educational needs policies, practices and patterns of provision and support in local education authorities. The combinations of criteria adopted, therefore, are meaningful only in their particular contexts.

- There is much emphasis on the importance of furthering educational psychology practices that are supported by relevant research evidence.

Appendix B:
RESPONSES TO THE DRAFT REPORT REPRINTED FROM THE *DECP NEWSLETTER* – August 1999

The DECP Working Party met for the first time in February 1998 and included representation from the Association of Educational Psychologists and the National Association of Principal Educational Psychologists. The remit of the Working Party was to review relevant research and practice in order to write a brief report to clarify the current concept of dyslexia, its links with literacy learning/difficulties and implications for educational psychology assessments. School-aged children were to be the primary focus of the report.

In January 1999 a draft report was circulated for consultation to all educational psychology services, members of the DECP, course tutors, researchers with expertise in this field and others with a particular interest in the topic. In this article we summarise the views of the respondents and consider their implications for the final version of the report.

RESPONSES RECEIVED

We would like to start by thanking all those who responded to the consultation. We know that the questions we asked and, indeed, the topic itself, demanded considerable time and effort from psychologists meeting as services or in groups to discuss the report or to respond as individuals or on behalf of educational psychology services. The present short account cannot do justice to the expertise of our audiences and all the helpful comments that we received. We hope that the suggested amendments will be evident in the revised report.

The total number of responses received was 214 and included 31 in the form of letters rather than completed questionnaires. This article considers primarily the 183 questionnaire responses. Of these, 141 were received from practising educational psychologists (EPs), senior educational psychologists (SEPs) and principal educational psychologists (PEPs) in local authority educational psychology services from 84 LEA services in England, Wales and Northern Ireland. We do not know how many educational psychologists in total were involved in the consultation as the collective responses or the responses on behalf of services did not usually state this. The designations of LEA respondents and a regional breakdown of the services involved are presented in Tables 1 and 2.

Table 1. Designation of LEA respondents

EP	SEP	PEP/Assist. PEP	Total
82 (58%)	33 (24%)	25 (18%)	141

Table 2. Number of LEAs represented by the responses

England	London Boroughs	Wales	Northern Ireland	Total
56 (67%)	17 (20%)	8 (9%)	3 (4%)	84

Completed questionnaires were also received from 42 respondents (23 per cent of the sample of 183) representing other contexts. Of these, 16 (9 per cent) were educational psychologists working as self-employed and/or retired; 13 (7 per cent) were lecturers in higher or further education; 8 (4 per cent) researchers in cognitive psychology with particular expertise in this field; and 5 (3 per cent) responses were written on behalf of organisations such as the Association of Educational Psychologists (AEP).

What is not directly included in the present account are the views and suggestions emanating from meetings that we held with educational psychologists (e.g. during the DECP Annual Course), trainee educational psychologists, students and teachers. We also actively sought the views of cognitive psychologists with expertise in literacy research and are particularly grateful for their comments regarding the academic content.

THE VIEWS OF RESPONDENTS

Having attempted separate analyses for different subgroups of respondents (e.g. those written on behalf of services, those not in LEA employment), it became clear to us that the over-all trend for the 'yes/no' questions was very similar across all groupings. Consequently, this article presents a single analysis of quantitative results across the 183 completed questionnaires. We start by providing data for the questions that we asked in the consultation. The comments then focus primarily on the responses expressing concerns and the improvements that can be made in order to clarify or amplify or adjust the report. The final section considers implications for the revised report.

THE WORDS DYSLEXIA OR DYSLEXIC

The draft report outlined the history of the word 'dyslexia' within a wider cultural context. The term had become established in popular language and was often used synonymously with or as a subset of 'specific learning difficulties'. Our survey of educational psychology practice indicated that debate about terminology was no longer a central issue. In cognitive research, dyslexia had for many years been a short-hand for marked difficulties with the reading and writing of an alphabetic script.

Proposal for practice

It was proposed that we use the word 'dyslexia' either synonymously with 'specific learning difficulties or as a subset of 'specific learning difficulties' concerned with literacy.

Questions for consultation	Yes	No	No response	Total
Do you support the use of 'dyslexia'	130 (71%)	28 (15%)	25 (14%)	183
Synonymously with SpLD	41 (22%)	109 (60%)	33 (18%)	183
As a subset of SpLD	120 (66%)	33 (18%)	30 (16%)	183

Comments

Although there was majority support for the use of 'dyslexia' this did not necessarily imply a sense of enthusiasm about the term. Views are perhaps best illustrated by the following quote: 'We don't support or not support the use of 'dyslexia'. We now accept the argument is probably not useful.' The responses also tended to regard 'dyslexia' as a subset of specific learning difficulties rather than being synonymous with it.

There was concern by some about the use of terminology that seemed to imply a focus on within-child causative factors rather than effective teaching and inclusive practices. Conversely, our emphasis on dyslexia as a mainstream issue worried those who feared that serious problems could be overlooked.

Another concern was that society would continue to define dyslexia in a different fashion rather than in the way suggested by the report. As this is already happening, educational psychologists have a choice of avoiding the term or taking a pro-active role in informing society of the meaning that psychological research and practice gives it.

Some who wished to avoid the term suggested synonyms such as 'literacy difficulties', 'specific literacy difficulties' (from the AEP), 'persistent and severe literacy difficulties' and 'learning difficulties in literacy'. With this caveat, the respondents agreed with much of the content of the report.

A WORKING DEFINITION OF DYSLEXIA

Sections 2.4 and 2.5 of the draft report argued that, for the purposes of scientific clarity, we needed an operational definition of dyslexia that excluded causal explanations. The definition should be descriptive with no explanatory elements. It should focus on positive identifying characteristics rather than exclusionary criteria.

Proposal for practice

It was proposed that we use the following working definition as a starting point for assessment and for the generation and testing of multivariate explanations drawing on psychological theory and research:

> *Dyslexia is evident when fluent and accurate word identification (reading) and/or spelling does not develop or does so very incompletely or with great difficulty.*

Questions for consultation	Yes	No	No response	Total
Do you support the use of a working definition that separates description from causal explanations?	130 (71%)	28 (15%)	25 (14%)	183

Which of these working definitions do you prefer:

Alternative A: *Dyslexia is evident when fluent and accurate word identification (reading) and/or spelling does not develop or does so very incompletely or with great difficulty.*

Alternative B: *Dyslexia is evident when fluent and accurate word identification (reading) and/or spelling develops very incompletely or with great difficulty.*

Alternative A	Alternative B	Neither	No response	Total
27 (15%)	108 (59%)	15 (8%)	33 (18%)	183

Comments

It is clear that a very substantial majority supported the use of a working definition that separated description from causal explanations. It can also be seen that Alternative B was preferred. The use of a working definition was also acceptable to those replacing 'dyslexia' with 'literacy difficulties'. Comments showed, however, that respondents wished to delimit the working definition further and to include more reference to learning opportunities. Consequently, in the final section of this article, we shall consider an amended working definition.

DYSLEXIA IN THE CONTEXT OF SKILLED READING AND SPELLING

Section 3 of the draft report summarised current knowledge about the processes involved in reading and spelling. In the context of this information, dyslexia could be regarded as a function of the reciprocal effects of learning opportunities and the type and extent of phonological, orthographic and semantic strengths and difficulties.

Proposal for practice:

As part of initial training and continuing professional development, educational psychologists need to ensure that they keep up to date with developments in literacy research and practice.

Questions for consultation	Yes	No	No response	Total
Do you agree with the proposal?	174 (95%)	3 (2%)	6 (3%)	183
Does Section 3 require amendments?	32 (17%)	94 (52%)	57 (31%)	183

Comments

It would have been surprising if educational psychologists did not agree with this proposal. There were riders, however, such as the suggestion that we 'keep up to date as far as possible' in the light of the volume of research in this field. It was also suggested that we contribute to the research, particularly in relation to practice issues, rather than keep up with the research of others. Furthermore, the recommendation required readily available digests of current research such as the present report.

Section 3 was generally seen as 'impressive and ground-breaking' in having placed the consideration of dyslexia, and the associated causal hypotheses, firmly in the context of what we know about literacy development. Researchers with expertise in this field found the section accurate although there were differences of opinion as to the emphasis given to the 'connectionist model'. Those educational psychologists wishing for amendments were usually asking for more information, for example, in relation to spelling development. Some requested that the report be written in 'plainer' English emphasis given to the 'connectionist model'. Those educational

THEORETICAL EXPLANATIONS OF DYSLEXIA

Section 4 of the report considered different theoretical explanations of dyslexia in the light of what was known about literacy development. These theoretical explanations were expressed in the form of a series of hypotheses where each presented a particular kind of analysis that could contribute to our understanding of the individual case. While the explanations were not mutually exclusive, they stressed different aspects in a causal modelling framework involving biological, cognitive and behavioural levels of analysis. Some hypotheses were supported by a body of convincing research while others fared less well in the evaluations provided in this section.

Proposal for practice

Educational psychology assessments need to consider different hypotheses of dyslexia in order to evaluate interactive explanations in the individual case.

Questions for consultation	Yes	No	No response	Total
Do you agree with the proposal?	154 (84%)	17 (9%)	14 (7%)	183
Does Section 4 require amendments?	38 (21%)	87 (47%)	58 (32%)	183

Comments

This proposal also received clear majority support. There were worries, however, about the 'distal' theoretical nature of these hypotheses. Most of them did not link with 'proximal' evaluations of literacy progress or curriculum-based assessments that led to the planning of intervention. In the revised report we need to emphasise, therefore, that this section is a review and critique of different theories, not a recipe for assessment. Implications for educational psychology assessments are considered in the following section.

Suggestions for improvements came primarily from researchers with expertise in this field. They helped us develop the causal modelling framework further emphasising, in particular, the central role currently given to phonology. We have also added an account of research in the area of temporal processing.

A FRAMEWORK FOR ASSESSMENT AND INTERVENTION

The draft report built on publications that have provided guidance for educational psychology assessment and intervention in general (DECP, 1998) and statutory assessments in particular (AEP, 1998). These documents have emphasised the multifaceted nature of educational psychology assessment. Not only are individual and instructional but also social, motivational and organisational variables taken into account. The role of practitioners is to investigate a range of possible explanations, and their interactions, in order to test out hypotheses that can lead to workable plans of action.

Proposal for practice

Educational psychology assessments of dyslexia should have regard to the DECP draft framework for psychological assessment and intervention.

Questions for consultation	Yes	No	No response	Total
Do you agree with the proposal?	164 (90%)	9 (5%)	10 (5%)	183

Comments

While there was good agreement with this proposal, some pointed out that it was not the only framework. Also, some felt strongly that a framework should be regarded as useful guidance rather as a blueprint for practice.

A NETWORK OF RECIPROCAL EFFECTS

Section 5.3 of the draft report noted that cognitive mechanisms underpinning literacy could also involve other areas of development such as certain skills in mathematics. While comprehensive assessment would consider all relevant areas of learning, the working definition implied that dyslexia could not be identified through an examination of associated difficulties alone. It was suggested that assessment should start from the examination of word reading and spelling and then move on to consider influencing factors. Table 5.1 showed the network of reciprocal effects between learning opportunities, teaching methods and individual cognitive make-up that could impact on reading and spelling.

Proposal for practice

Individual assessment starts with an analysis of the child's reading and spelling performance in the context of their pedagogical experiences.

Questions for consultation	Yes	No	No response	Total
Do you agree with the proposal?	160 (87%)	13 (7%)	10 (6%)	183
Do you agree with the suggestions in Table 5.1?	141 (77%)	18 (10%)	24 (13%)	183

Comments

There was again high agreement with the proposal and the suggestions in Table 1. Some felt that the wider context needed to be investigated first and wished to replace 'starts' with 'includes'. A greater emphasis on the child's views and experiences and the essential partnership with parents was also highlighted. Although there was agreement with Table 5.1, many found it rather wordy. We shall try to revise and shall certainly replace 'pedagogical' with 'teaching and learning'.

SOCIAL POLICY

The draft report considered issues of administrative practice in relation to legislation (DfEE, 1994; DfEE, 1996; DfEE, 1997) and concluded that there was no ready formula to link a particular pattern or level of dyslexic difficulty to a particular formulation of learning difficulty or provision. Section 5.8 and Figure 5.1 showed that the working definition may also provide a starting point for social policy decisions. The definitional features, which exist as continua, could justify different aspects of the educational psychologist's role. Educational psychologists can work with schools to develop effective school-based assessment, intervention and monitoring and, within that context, carry out detailed psychological assessment and programme planning to promote the progress of those children whose difficulties are most severe and persistent. This way of working is in accordance with the recommendations of the Green Paper, *Excellence for All Children* (DfEE, 1997).

Proposal for practice

We propose that the working definition, which focuses on the extent, severity and persistence of difficulties with word identification (reading) and spelling, provides a starting point for social policy decisions.

Questions for consultation	Yes	No	No response	Total
Do you agree with the proposal?	153 (83%)	14 (8%)	16 (9%)	183
Does Figure 5.1 require amendments?	37 (20%)	94 (52%)	52 (28%)	183

Comments

Use of the working definition as a starting point for social policy developments received a high level of support. Many said, however, that more emphasis needed to be placed on assessing the learning environment. This led to the central issue identified by both academics and practitioners – the evaluation of intervention as a measure of persistence.

Some argued that social policy was influencing the working definition too much in Figure 5.1 and that social policy issues needed to be cross referenced to documents such as the Code of Practice and the National Literacy Strategy.

DYSLEXIA AS A MAINSTREAM ISSUE

The report stated that in all but exceptional circumstances dyslexia was catered for in mainstream schools without a statement of special educational needs (DfEE, 1994; DfEE, 1997, 1.14). Because the behavioural features of the present working definition existed on continua, the vast majority of dyslexic children would be supported within their mainstream schools with appropriate additional advice. With regard to early identification, section 5.9 suggested that teachers and carers notice children's individual needs and then adjust their responses accordingly. This interplay between 'noticing' and 'adjusting' seemed the most appropriate basis for monitoring the progress of young children at risk of reading failure.

Proposal for practice

We propose that educational psychologists work in collaboration with teachers and carers to develop approaches and skills so that individual needs can be noticed from an early stage and teaching adjusted to accommodate these needs.

Question for consultation

In your view, how can educational psychologists help teachers develop approaches to 'noticing and adjusting' within the context of the National Literacy Strategy?

Comments

We did not ask any direct yes/no questions here. But our formulation involving teachers and carers in *noticing* children's individual needs and then *adjusting* their responses accordingly was singled out as particularly valuable by those respondents who did not wish to use the word dyslexia and also by those who did (e.g. the British Dyslexia Association). This is an important way forward with many implications for practice.

We should probably not have requested suggestions or examples of practice in this context. As one respondent pointed out, it was surely the task of the working party to describe such practice. Nevertheless, copies of guidance for teachers were appended with some responses. It is clear that further work is needed in this area.

ASSESSING EXTENT, SEVERITY AND PERSISTENCE

The report argued that educational psychologists are well informed about the validity, reliability and appropriateness of particular measures of literacy. In determining the persistence of learning difficulties, they usually draw on the information provided by teachers, parents and the learners themselves. As shown in the reviews in Section 4.9, cognitive test batteries (e.g. BAS, WISC) can be informative when pointing to strengths and weaknesses in the individual case. However, no particular pattern of sub-test scores can be regarded as necessary or sufficient in deciding whether and to what extent learning difficulties can be described as dyslexic.

Proposal for practice

The importance ascribed to measures of extent, severity and persistence implies that educational psychologists become involved in research to develop more finely tuned tests of aspects such as reading accuracy, comprehension and rate, spelling accuracy, speed of writing and measures of rates of progress in response to intervention over time.

Questions for consultation	Yes	No	No response	Total
Do you support the proposal?	147 (80%)	11 (6%)	25 (14%)	183

Comments

While generally agreeing with the proposal, the main critique was that the proposal placed too much emphasis on psychometrics. The focus should be on the development of better ways for observing learning environments and evaluating interventions. The assessment-through-teaching approach, familiar to educational psychologists, was highlighted as a means by which systematic data on persistence as well as severity could be collected. Respondents wished to develop further approaches which were 'formative' rather than the 'summative' and linked with the National Curriculum and the National Literacy Strategy.

IMPLICATIONS FOR THE REVISED REPORT

In statistical terms, the draft report certainly has the support of the majority of respondents. Nevertheless, there are amendments and additions to be made in line with the suggestions received and the critique of particular aspects.

The first issue to consider is the use of the word 'dyslexia'. Although it has majority support, we acknowledge the concerns described earlier in this article. There is indeed no requirement to use the term as substitutes such as 'literacy difficulties' also recognise that some children experience serious problems in mastering the alphabetic script. The report will continue to refer to dyslexia as a shorthand for marked and persistent difficulties at the 'word level' of the National Literacy Strategy.

There is considerable support for a working definition that separates description from causal explanations (84 per cent) and for its use as a starting point for social policy decisions (83 per cent). Respondents emphasise, however, that the definition needs to include mention of learning opportunities. One possible form the revised working definition may take is as follows:

A WORKING DEFINITION OF DYSLEXIA

Dyslexia is evident when accurate and fluent word reading and/or spelling is learnt very incompletely or with great difficulty. The definition focuses on literacy learning at the 'word level' and implies that the problem is severe and persistent despite appropriate learning opportunities. It provides the basis for a staged process of assessment through teaching.

Sections 3 and 4 of the report are appreciated as informative and scholarly. In the current discussion of the future role of educational psychologists, the report provides an example of the way educational psychologists consider cognitive theory and research in relation to practice. Critique, however, focuses on the relevance of the information for educational practitioners. Two main points are made. First, most of the research does not currently have direct implications for curriculum-based assessment and intervention. Second, there needs to be a change of emphasis in the report away from within-child causative factors to the evaluation of children's responses to teaching methods and approaches.

The formulation of dyslexia as primarily a mainstream issue starts to address these points. Our suggestion that educational psychologists work with teachers and carers in order to help them *notice* children's individual needs and then *adjust* their responses accordingly is singled out as particularly valuable by those respondents who do not wish to use the word dyslexia and also by those who do. This way of thinking is indeed at the heart of inclusive practice and provides the basis for the kind of collaborative work, over time, that we believe is central in educational psychology.

It was not the remit of the working party to evaluate teaching methods or current interventions. In the revised report we shall nevertheless write a more substantial section that considers these issues in principle. What is now needed is further work in this area.

Appendix C:
PUBLISHED TESTS THAT DRAW ON THEORETICAL RATIONALES OF DYSLEXIA

NB: Appendix C should be read together with the full draft report entitled *Dyslexia, Literacy and Psychological Assessment*, **written by a Working Party of The British Psychological Society Division of Educational and Child Psychology.**

Appendix C evaluates a selection of commercially available tests designed to measure cognitive processes associated with dyslexia. As shown in the theoretical rationales described for each test, the measures reflect different hypotheses outlined in Section 4 of the full report. The evaluations show that some of the tests are better supported by current research than others and that information about their standardisation is also rather variable. The evaluations demonstrate that no one test can be considered obligatory in educational psychology assessments.

The selection of tests is not intended to be comprehensive but to give a flavour of the kinds of approaches available, their rationales, validities and implications for practice. The following tests are reviewed in the appendix:

1. **Aston Index**

2. **Bangor Dyslexia Test**

3. **Boder Test of Reading – Spelling Patterns**

4. **Children's Test of Nonword Repetition**

5. **Dyslexia Screening Test and Dyslexia Early Screening Test**

6. **Graded nonword Reading Test**

7. **Lucid Cognitive Profiling System (CoPS)**

8. **Phonological Abilities Test**

9. **Phonological Assessment Battery**

10. **Self-Perception Profile for Learning Disabled Students**

11. **Wechsler Intelligence Scale for Children: The ACID Profile**

12. **Wilkins Rate of Reading Test**

1. Aston Index (Revised)
Authors: M.J. Newton & M.E. Thompson
Publisher: Wisbeach: Learning Development Aids
Date of publication: 1982

Description

The Aston Index was designed for use by classroom teachers in identifying specific learning problems including dyslexia. The tests are organised into two groups: Level 1 is for screening children who have been at school for about six months; Level 2 is for children over 7 years who are not making satisfactory progress with literacy skills. The tests comprising the Index are as follows.

✦ General underlying ability and attainment tests: Picture recognition (Level 1 only); vocabulary scale (Level 1 and 2); 'Goodenough draw-a-man-test'(Level 1 and 2); copying geometric designs (Level 1 and 2); Schonell reading test (Level 2 only); spelling test (Level 2 only).

✦ Performance items: laterality (Level 1 and 2); copying name (Level 1 only); free writing (Level 2 only); visual sequential memory – pictures (Level 1 and 2); auditory sequential memory (Level 1 and 2); visual sequential memory – symbolic (Level 1 and 2); sound discrimination (Level 1 and 2); grapheme/phoneme correspondence (Level 2 only); graphomotor test (Level 2 only).

The vocabulary scale and the Goodenough test produce scores that are considered to be 'mental age' scores and examples are provided in the manual where these are compared with a child's chronological age in categorising the children as 'slow learning' or 'in the above average range of intelligence'. The Schonell reading test and the spelling test result in 'attainment age' scores.

Theoretical rationale

The rationale for the Aston Index (as presented on page 1 of the Manual, and by Newton & Thompson, 1979a) is based on a diagnostic-prescriptive approach to reading difficulties. Reading, writing and spelling are hypothesised to be underpinned by a set of key skills: perception (auditory and visual), memory (auditory and visual), association of visual symbols with an event or idea, association of sound and symbol, orientation, left to right sequencing, graphomotor skills. It is argued that inadequate development of any one of these skills can result in difficulties in literacy acquisition. Overall the test seems rather dated. As considered in Section 4.6 of the main report, there is now little theoretical support for the relevance of tests involving visual sequential memory and the significance of mixed laterality has also been questioned by one of the designers of this test (Thompson, 1975).

Empirical status

Sutherland and Smith (1991) studied the use of the Aston Index as a dyslexia screening test with 11-12 year olds who had been identified as having reading difficulties. Of the five performance tests recorded on the profile they found that only the test of auditory sequential memory highlighted a substantial number of pupils with a difficulty. Scores on the other tests showed substantial ceiling effects. Sutherland and Smith (1991) conclude that the test has serious limitations when used with pupils in the 11+ age range and they note that pupils of secondary age were not included in the initial validation of the test. This is in contrast to the test manual which states that the index has been used successfully with older children and young adults and that, apart from the 'general underlying ability' tests, 'the other tests relate very satisfactorily to the older age range', (p.3).

Sutherland and Smith (1991) also conclude that the Aston Index is difficult to interpret. Age norm score profiles are provided for children aged 5.5 years, 7.5 years and 9.5 years so that the graphed profile for an individual can be compared to the closest age norm. Sutherland and Smith consider that the provision of score ranges that are one and two standard deviations from the mean would be less potentially misleading. They note that the Aston Index and the Boder Test showed considerable agreement on the pupils identified as having auditory processing problems, despite the very different approaches and materials used by the two tests. They conclude however that the Boder Test is to be preferred.

Pumfrey (1985) is critical of the information given in the manual on the construction, standardisation and validation of the Aston Index, which he describes as 'meagre'. In particular he notes that the size and characteristics of the samples are not given in reporting concurrent and predictive validity data. While this information is published elsewhere (Newton & Thompson, 1979b; Newton, Thompson & Richards, 1979), these studies are not referenced in the Manual.

McGhee (1996) also criticises the construction and standardisation of the Aston Index, but considers that selected tests can be helpful in profiling strengths and weaknesses. Stackhouse and Wells (1997) take a similar approach in suggesting the use of the Aston Index Sound Blending test from their examination of available tests that tap phonological processing skills.

Implications for practice

Scores on tests 10 to 14 are plotted on a profile and guidance is given on profiles indicative of dyslexia. This guidance is based on illustrative case study reports and no information is provided on its research basis. While particular tests may be valuable for investigating various aspects of a child's functioning, there are questions about the construction, standardisation and validation of the Index as a whole.

The user is directed towards intervention materials linked to the areas tested in the Index (in particular those contained in the Aston Portfolio). However, as Pumfrey (1985) points out, evidence on the efficacy of this particular diagnostic teaching approach is not provided.

2. Bangor Dyslexia Test
Author: T.R. Miles
Publisher: Learning Development Aids
First published 1983; second edition 1997

Description

This test is administered individually as part of a clinical interview. It involves looking for positive indicators of a syndrome of dyslexia through the following 10 items: Left-right (body parts); repeating polysyllabic words; subtraction; tables; reciting months forwards; reciting months in reversed order; reciting digits forward; reciting digits in reversed order; b-d confusion; familial incidence. The test should not be given to pupils under the age of seven years.

Theoretical rationale

The manual states that the test is 'offered not as a means of definitive diagnosis, but rather as a contribution towards further understanding of the subject's strengths and weaknesses' (p.5). The theoretical basis draws on the syndrome hypothesis introduced by Miles in the early 1980s and described in Section 4.8 of this report. The theory assumes that symptoms and signs with a hereditary component are related to reading and spelling competence and also to other areas of functioning. These symptoms and signs can be understood in terms of deficits in verbal labelling/working memory processes (Miles, 1993).

Empirical status

Technical details are provided in Miles (1993), not the manual. The items comprising the test were developed from clinical data with some 291 subjects attending the University of Bangor clinic from 1972 to 1978. In terms of test standardisation theory, the Bangor Dyslexia Test cannot be considered a psychometric instrument. The clinical and cumulative nature of Miles's work was not intended for this purpose and, as discussed below, interpretation of test items depends much more on 'clinical judgement' than the particular number of 'dyslexia positive' scores obtained by the individual. Clinical judgements can of course differ amongst the practitioners involved. Unlike tests specific to a particular language, the items in the Bangor Test can be translated and tried out in other countries. Appendices in Miles (1993) contain versions in Greek, German and Japanese but do not provide data about their use or validation in these countries.

Implications for practice

This test will interest those wishing to consider a syndrome hypothesis as defined by Miles (1993). Miles cautions, however, against uncritical use of the test scores. He states that the scores can be a guide only and that practitioners may prefer to rely on their overall clinical impressions. In this sense the test is not really a test but a means for systematic observation and comparison of the judgements of those involved. For this reason, it is important to refer extensively to the theoretical discussion of each item provided in Miles (1993). As one approach amongst other possibilities, the test should not be used in isolation from relevant information about educational achievements and instructional approaches.

3. Boder Test of Reading-Spelling Patterns
Authors: E. Boder & S. Jerrico
Publisher: Grune and Stratton, USA
Date of publication: 1982

Description

This test is based on the clinical work undertaken by a paediatric neurologist and a research psychologist in Los Angeles. Although the work took place in the US, the test has also attracted interest in this country (Reason, 1984; Sutherland & Smith, 1991). Designed for use with subjects aged from five years to adulthood, it is more suitable for older children with a sufficient level of reading and spelling to be able to attempt the test items.

The test consists of an oral word reading test, derived from a series of graded word lists, and a spelling test based on the results of the reading test. The word lists for reading consist of either phonetically regular or irregular words. They are presented in two ways, either 'flash' which gives one second for each word or 'untimed' allowing up to ten seconds for phonic analysis of the word. The spelling tests also consist of phonetically regular and irregular words. They are constructed so that one list contains words that the subject could read in the reading test (known words) and the other words that the subject could not read so enabling scoring according to good phonetic equivalence of the target word. Adequate administration of the test requires considerable practice. There may be variability, for example, in assessing what constitutes 'good phonetic equivalence' in spelling.

Theoretical rationale

The rationale of the test is taken from a reading disability typology introduced by Boder in the 1960s (see also Section 4.10) . On the basis of the pattern of performance obtained, those with literacy difficulties are identified in terms of three subtypes. The dysphonetic group is by far the largest, defined as containing subjects who have difficulty integrating visual symbols with their sounds, i.e. phonic word-analysis skills. A minority of children are classed as belonging to the dyseidetic group manifesting weaknesses in visual perception and memory for letters and whole-word configurations. The third dysphonetic-dyseidetic group combine both kinds of deficits.

Empirical status

The authors have determined differential identification of reading-spelling patterns through cut-off performance scores on the tests. Test-retest reliabilities for the classification of 50 subjects aged between six and 15 years are reported as consistently high. The test can be criticised, however, on technical grounds in relation to item selection and cut-off criteria on which little information is provided (Pumfrey, 1985). According to Reynolds (1986), the Boder Test is a valuable heuristic that has failed when translated into a practical assessment tool, primarily because of a lack of attention to the psychometric aspects of the test.

Evidence for the validity of the subtypes is considered in the test manual with reference to four PhD theses supervised by the authors prior to the publication of the test. However, subsequent research (Nockleby & Galbraith, 1984; Van-den-Bos, 1984) and more recent PhD theses (Bedi, 1994; Miller, 1994) do not provide support to the premise that there are subtypes characterised by opposite patterns of strengths and weaknesses within the auditory and visual processing channels.

The field of research concerned with subtypes that differentiate between phonological and orthographic coding is reviewed by Stanovich *et al.* (1997). The authors conclude that comparisons involving reading age rather than chronological age matched controls demonstrate that phonological dyslexia remains a robust subtype while visual (surface) dyslexia is very infrequent.

Implications for practice

A test that compares 'flash' and 'untimed' word reading seems intuitively attractive to those interested in examining the fluency and automaticity of word recognition skills as included in the working definition of this report. Similarly, the investigation of spelling in terms of the dichotomies of phonologically regular/irregular words, which the subject can/cannot read, provides interesting information with apparent face validity. However, as Boder's classification system and the test standardisation data now seem dated, the normative information is not directly applicable. In terms of teaching implications, the manual recommends a systematic phonic approach regardless of subtype.

4. Children's Test of Nonword Repetition
Authors: S.E. Gathercole & A.D. Baddeley
Publisher: The Psychological Corporation
Date of Publication: 1996

Description

This is a test of short term (or 'working') memory standardised with children aged between four and eight years. It consists of 40 nonwords (such as 'depelate', 'skiticult') presented on the accompanying audio cassette tape. The child is asked to repeat each nonword and the tester judges the accuracy of each response.

Theoretical rationale

A body of research has established that nonword repetition provides a sensitive measure of short term memory skills (Gathercole, Willis, Baddeley & Emslie, 1994). As discussed in section 4.5 of this report, adequate short term memory is required if children are to blend and build the component sounds of letters in unfamiliar words.

This test complements those specifically designed to tap aspects of phonological processing where phonological working memory is an implicit, but not explicitly measured, component of the test items. The authors refer to evidence showing that performance on the test of nonword repetition is more closely linked to reading achievement than measures of digit span. The test also reflects more general problems in language development not considered in the present review.

Empirical status

Standardisation data is reported for a sample of 612 children with a minimum of 84 children for each of the five age levels (ages 4 to 8). The test was administered to children in Cambridgeshire, Lancashire and Cumbria. While the schools were located in a range of urban, suburban and rural areas, no mention is made of the composition of the sample in terms of gender or cultural background. Studies of test-retest and split-half reliability provide good coefficients ranging from 0.66 to 0.77. Validity is demonstrated through two relatively small studies involving correlations with a single word reading test. The authors also report an unpublished study showing that children aged 6-16 attending the Dyslexia Institute consistently underperform on the test (Turner, 1995).

Implications for practice

The link between short term memory and reading development may be important for practitioners. As nonword repetition is a purely verbal task, it does not involve exposing children to print and thus has wide applicability. It is argued that the unfamiliar spoken items do not disadvantage children with less rich environmental experience of language. What is required, however, is further research on the applicability of the test for children in the UK whose home language is not English. With regard to older learners with literacy difficulties, the test can provide useful information bearing in mind that the instructions were designed for young children.

5. Dyslexia Screening Test (DST) and Dyslexia Early Screening Test (DEST)
Authors: R. Nicolson & A. Fawcett
Publisher: The Psychological Corporation
Date of publication: 1996

Description

The DST is designed to be administered by a teacher or psychologist, taking about 30 minutes per child. It is normed for children from age 6.5 to 16.5 years. It comprises 11 subtests, of which three are attainment tests of reading, writing and spelling fluency. The other 'diagnostic' tests measure naming speed, phonological skill, memory, motor skill, balance, temporal processing, and verbal/ semantic fluency. The test yields an overall 'at risk' score together with a profile of abilities.

The DEST is similar to the DST but normed for children from age 4.5 to 6.5 years. It comprises 10 subtests, of which two are tests of letter and digit knowledge. The others measure naming speed, phonological skill, memory, motor skill, balance, temporal processing, and shape copying ability. This test, also, yields an overall 'at risk' score together with a profile of abilities.

Theoretical rationale

The authors of DST and DEST aim to provide a test battery which furnishes a set of positive 'at risk' indicators for dyslexia. These indicators include the dyslexia identifying features of various kinds of difficulty in the areas of reading, writing and spelling. They also include causal factors of dyslexia in the areas of phonological skill and the development of fluency (including motor fluency).

The inclusion of the balance and motor tasks in the test batteries reflects the view that dyslexia, mediated by a general skill automatisation deficit, involves underlying minor functional abnormalities of the cerebellum (see Section 4.3; Nicolson & Fawcett, 1995; Fawcett, Nicolson & Dean, 1996). It is important that psychologists are aware of the full theoretical rationale underpinning these items.

Empirical status

The DST and DEST batteries take account of the evidence that dyslexic individuals have problems in tasks that require the processing of phonological information (Snowling, 1995; Nicolson, 1996). They go beyond this, however, by testing for the presence of deficits in balance, which may share a common underlying cause (cerebellar malfunction) with other related deficits (e.g. Nicolson, Fawcett & Dean, 1995). Evidence of the discriminatory power of the DST and DEST is based on the authors' own research (e.g. Nicolson & Fawcett, 1990, 1994a, 1995). According to the authors, dyslexic children have significantly worse performance than reading age controls across a wide range of tests of primitive skills. The investigation of links between these and other kinds of deficit (e.g. time estimation) is an area of active research (Nicolson, 1996).

Implications for practice

The DST and DEST are recently published tests providing a biological conceptual basis. The tests can provide one strategy for early identification. However, practitioners should separate judgements of 'at risk' from the judgements involved in the identification of dyslexia and the administrative processes that determine special educational needs. It is also necessary to guard against making any categorical statements about an individual's neuro-psychological functioning on the basis of DST/ DEST results alone.

The DST subtests seek to elicit contrasts between the child's verbal and semantic fluency on the basis that 'dyslexic people often have considerable strengths which may offset their weaknesses' (Fawcett & Nicolson, 1996, p.8). It may be questioned, however, whether the lack of such contrasts, like any other exclusionary criteria, should influence interpretation or scoring of dyslexia risk assessment. It is worth noting that the DST authors themselves observe that investigation of some strengths may be difficult to achieve in a short screening test of this type. The tests reflect the theoretical stance developed by the authors. Independent validation by other researchers is not yet available.

6. Graded Nonword Reading Test
Authors: M J Snowling, S. E. Stothard & J. McClean
Publisher: Thames Valley Test Company, Bury St Edmunds, England
Date of publication: 1996

Description

The Graded Nonword Reading Test is an individually administered test that examines the ability to read nonwords (novel letter strings that represent plausible word pronunciations in the English language, but which do not actually exist in the English lexicon). The test consists of five practice items followed by ten single syllable and ten two syllable nonwords. Acceptable pronunciations for each nonword are provided, with a helpful pronunciation guide. Regional variations in the pronunciation of vowel sounds are allowed. Each nonword is presented singly, page by page, in large type in the test booklet. Administration and scoring of the test takes in total around five minutes. 10th, 25th, 50th and 75th centile equivalents for raw scores are provided for both chronological age and for British Ability Scales word reading age bands. The test is designed for use primarily with children between the ages of 6 years and 11 years. According to the authors, the test can also be used with weak readers older than the chronological age bands provided.

Theoretical rationale

The test assumes that, in learning to read, children must map letter-strings onto their most probable pronunciation. In the case of two syllable nonwords, this also requires an awareness of the most probable and lawful point at which the first syllable ends and the second syllable starts. Nonword reading provides a test of word decoding when other aids to decoding, such as lexical knowledge, are excluded.

Individuals identified as dyslexic tend to be poorer at nonword decoding than reading-age matched controls (see Rack, Snowling & Olson, 1992, for a review). Case examples in an appendix provide illustrations of dyslexic learners, approaching functional word reading levels, who tend to rely more extensively on orthographic and semantic information than phonological information. Exploration of an individual's nonword reading, in comparison to reading comprehension and word reading levels, can therefore be useful.

Empirical status

The graded nonword reading test was standardised, between 1990 and 1993 with 653 children aged 5 to 11 years, drawn from three regions of England. Each child was also given the British Ability Scales Word Reading Test. An appendix provides further standardisation data with a sample of 357 children in relation to the Schonell Graded Word Reading Test.

Guidelines for interpretation are appropriately conservative and cautious, and in psychometric terms the Graded Nonword Reading Test appears to be sound. Although all the test items correspond with plausible pronunciations, no rationale is given as to why the particular items were chosen, for instance, in terms of the internal letter string structure, or orthographic or phonological similarities to real words.

The manual gives details of internal and test-retest reliability, and concurrent validity in terms of correlations between test performance and performance on the British Ability Scales word reading test. The test is also reported to discriminate between a small group of identified dyslexic children and chronological and reading age match controls. Although group means are given, confirming poorer performance on the nonword reading test compared to a word reading test, it is also evident that some of the children identified as dyslexic can read nonwords at an equivalent level to their real word reading.

Implications for practice

The manual stresses that scores should be interpreted conservatively and alongside other details of literacy performance. As the test is not timed, it will not discriminate between individuals who rapidly and automatically map the nonword letter strings onto pronunciations from those who complete the task more slowly by a process of phonological assembly. In the latter case, the slowness of an individual's performance may provide qualitative evidence alongside other observations. Particularly with older learners, who have started to acquire a more functional word reading age, poor performance on this test relative to word reading might be seen as a fairly strong indicator of underlying dyslexic reading difficulties. Clearly, however, such interpretation should be supported with other evidence.

7. Lucid Cognitive Profiling System (CoPS)
Authors: C.H. Singleton, K.V. Thomas & R.C. Leedale
Publisher: Lucid Research, Beverley, East Yorkshire
Date of publication: 1996

Description

CoPS Cognitive Profiling System is a computer-based standardised assessment system for use by teachers or psychologists with children aged 4:0 a fairly strong indicator of underlying dyslexic reading difficulties. Clearly, however, such interpretation shof children who are at risk of literacy difficulties or dyslexia, and helps teachers to recognise children's learning styles. The tests are presented as 'games', which facilitates maintenance of attention. A graphical profile of results is automatically calculated, displayed (in centile or z-score format) and may be printed out. CoPS is available for Windows or Acorn multimedia computers, and the suite comprises eight main tests and one supplementary test, as follows: Visual/verbal sequential memory (colours) *Zoid's Friends*; Visual sequential memory (spatial and temporal) *Rabbits*; Visual/verbal associative memory (shape and colour) *Toybox*; Visual /verbal sequential memory (symbols) *Zoid's Letters*; Auditory/verbal associative memory (symbols and names) *Zoid's Letter Names*; Auditory/verbal sequential memory (names) *Races*; Phonological awareness (rhyming and alliteration) *Rhymes*;

Auditory discrimination *Wock*; Colour discrimination (supplementary test) *Clown*.

Theoretical rationale

The theoretical rationale behind CoPS is that phonological awareness, memory ability and auditory discrimination are critical determinants of early literacy development and, consequently, children who struggle with reading or writing are likely to have weaknesses in these cognitive abilities. Early assessment of cognitive skills can therefore have predictive value for the teacher or psychologist. The aim is to assist teachers to differentiate teaching so that it addresses individual learning needs more appropriately, before the child experiences failure in literacy development.

Empirical status

The research behind CoPS included a five-year longitudinal study of 400 children in 24 schools carried out by psychologists at the University of Hull. The final tests in the suite were selected from a total of 27 different prototypes on the basis of predictive accuracy and reliability. The eight main tests in CoPS have all been shown, independently and in combination, to have significant correlations with later literacy development. The highest correlations between the CoPS tests at five years and reading ability at age eight were in auditory sequential memory ($r = 0.56$), phonological awareness ($r = 0.52$), auditory discrimination ($r = 0.44$) and visual/verbal sequential memory ($r = 0.39$). Phonic skills at age eight also correlated significantly with these measures, with the highest correlation coefficient being 0.73 for auditory discrimination. Stepwise multiple regression analyses showed that the phonological awareness and auditory sequential memory tests administered at age 5 together accounted for 48 per cent of the variance in reading ability at age 8 (compared with only 23 per cent of the variance being attributable to verbal intelligence). In discriminant function analysis, with CoPS tests administered at age 5 and reading assessed at age 8, the overall prediction of poor readers was found to be 96 per cent, with a false negative rate of 16.7 per cent and a false positive rate of only 2.3 per cent.

Implications for practice

The administration of the CoPS tests can be supervised by a classroom assistant. The full suite takes a total of about 45 minutes to administer and can be done through several shorter sessions. Interpretation of the results from CoPS requires expertise in education or educational psychology. Training sessions on test administration and profile interpretation are available and the programme includes a teacher's manual that contains guidance for practitioners.

8. Phonological Abilities Test
   ### Authors: V. Muter, C. Hulme & M. Snowling
   ### Publisher: The Psychological Corporation
   ### Date of publication: 1997

Description

The test contains four phonological awareness subtests (rhyme detection, rhyme production, word completion, phoneme deletion), a speech rate subtest (repeating words as quickly as possible) and a letter knowledge subtest. The test is recommended for use with children aged 5-7 years.

Theoretical rationale

The test is based on the evidence that has accumulated over the past 30 years to show that children's phonological skills predict early reading progress. The authors refer, in particular, to children's ability to reflect upon and manipulate sounds in spoken words (phonological awareness) and their knowledge of letter names and sounds. The speech rate subtest is an innovative addition and draws on the research by McDougall, Hulme, Ellis and Monk (1994) which found that children's scores on a speech rate test were a better predictor of reading skill than a measure of short-term memory.

Empirical status

Standardisation data, reported in the manual, has been obtained by administering the test to 826 children aged 4-8. Only small samples were involved for the age ranges 4.00-4.11 and 7.06-7.11, making the test mainly suitable for 5-7 year olds. As the testing was undertaken by students at the University of York in their home towns, the standardisation can be regarded as representing an 'opportunity sample' rather than a nationally representative sample. However, as the subtests are well known items in cognitive research, the data can be regarded as sufficient for applied practice. The manual reports studies of reliability and validity which show that some subtests provide more robust data than others. The authors rightly suggest caution in interpreting results. It seems essential that users of the test familiarise themselves with the standardisation research in order to know what applied significance to ascribe to particular subtest scores. This information is not included in the interpretation of results section of the manual.

Implications for practice

The test is primarily intended as an instrument for noticing children who are 'at risk' of reading failure because of their slower phonological development. As such it is a useful indicator of the instructional emphasis required by these children. Of particular importance to practitioners is that the manual does not make reference to the term 'dyslexia' in the context of these younger children. It states, however, that the test can also be used with older children experiencing reading difficulties in order to assess the nature and extent of their phonological weaknesses and refers to studies demonstrating dyslexic children's difficulties with phonological skills. Bearing in mind that the test was designed to be attractive to young children, the materials may not appeal to older learners and standardisation data is not available for older age groups.

9. Phonological Assessment Battery (PhAB).
Authors: Frederickson, N., Frith, U. & Reason, R.
Publisher: Windsor: NFER-Nelson.
Date of publication: 1997

Description

This battery of tests is designed for use by psychologists, special educational needs co-ordinators in schools and speech therapists to assess phonological processing. It comprises the following tests: Alliteration, naming speed, rhyme, spoonerisms, rhyme and alliteration fluency and nonword reading.

Theoretical rationale

The theoretical rationale and research basis of the PhAB tests is discussed in detail in

Appendix 1 of the Manual. The authors draw on the extensive literature indicating an important relationship between phonological processing ability and the development of literacy skills. They also describe Frith's (1995) theoretical framework which formed the conceptual basis for test development and guided the construction of tests to assess different aspects of phonological processing skill. Interested readers are referred to a special edition of *Educational and Child Psychology* (Vol. 12, No. 1, 1995), for a detailed discussion of specific issues in relation to the construction of each test.

Empirical status

The tests were administered by NFER to a representative national sample of 629 pupils aged 6 years to 14 years 11 months. The standardisation and norms are presented in the manual. The manual contains technical data (relating to test standardisation, reliability and validity) and advice on test interpretation and individual programme planning. It also includes reports on two special studies, one with 89 children who have SpLD statements and the other with 50 children whose first language is Sylheti. The results of the first study offered support for the validity of the PhAB tests in that they showed that Children with SpLD achieved significantly lower scores on the PhAB tests than a representative sample of children of the same age and that the incidence of phonological difficulties was significantly higher among the SpLD group. The results of the second study suggest that PhAB may be an appropriate assessment technique to use with bilingual children as they indicated similar levels of performance and a similar relationship between phonological skills and reading in age-matched samples of monolingual and bilingual children.

Implications for practice

A study by Frederickson and Wilson (1996) of the effects of a Rhyme analogy training programme reported improvement, relative to controls, on those PhAB tests which involve rhyme generation. This suggests that the PhAB tests are sensitive to the effects of intervention and may have value in programme evaluation.

The manual gives information on test interpretation and programme planning. There is some support for the effectiveness of the phonological skills training suggested in improving both phonological and literacy skills which is congruent with other findings in the research literature. However, the authors strongly emphasise the importance of a balanced approach to literacy development within which phonological skills are but one, albeit important, component.

The test battery has been standardised on a representative sample and initial indications are that it can be used appropriately with pupils whose first language is not English. However, it is comparatively recently published and empirical studies are as yet sparse.

10. Self-Perception Profile for Learning Disabled Students
Authors: M.J. Renick & S. Harter
Publisher: University of Denver.
Date of publication: 1997

Description

The Self-Perception Profile is a self-report measure designed to assess children's judgements of their competence in particular areas and their perceived worth or esteem as a person. It is an adaptation for children with leaning disabilities (SpLD) of Harter's well researched Self Perception Profile for Children and can also be used with normally achieving children. The self report questionnaire consists of 46 items, organised into 10 sub-scales or domains which question students about the following aspects: the extent to which they perceive themselves to be 'smart', to be good readers, to be doing well at spelling, to be able to write good sentences to create a story, to understand maths, to feel accepted or popular among their peers, to feel competent at athletic activities, to like the way they behave, to feel happy with the way they look and to like themselves as a person.

Theoretical rationale

The manual details the rationale and research basis of the measure. It is based on Harter's developmental theory of the self which holds that children distinguish between a global perception of their worth as a person and their self-perception in relation to various competence domains in their lives (e.g. scholastic competence or athletic competence). The number of such domains increases with age as children's self-perceptions become increasingly differentiated.

It is argued that the social comparison processes engaged in by children with specific learning difficulties can lead to further differentiation of self-perceptions. Rennick and Harter report that children with SpLD differentiate between items on the 'Scholastic' scale of the original Self Perception Profile for Children, making a distinction (not found with normally achieving children) between their perceptions of their general intellectual ability and their performance at specific academic tasks. Hence the first five scales of the Self-Perception Profile for Learning Disabled Students replace the scholastic competence scale.

Empirical status

The manual contains data from the standardisation of the instrument with 201 SpLD pupils aged 9 to 13 years (90 of whom were in resourced mainstream provision and 111 of whom were in special schools) and 367 mainstream peers of the 90 SpLD pupils in resourced mainstream schools. Among the data reported for the SpLD and the mainstream groups are the internal consistency reliabilities of each scale, the factor patterns obtained, intercorrelations among the subscales and the means and standard deviations by scale and year group. Guidance is offered on the interpretation of individual children's scores.

While the Self Perception Profile for Children has been extensively used in research (including research with children who have SpLD, e.g. Bear, Clever & Proctor, 1991), data on the Self-Perception Profile for Learning Disabled Students is as yet less comprehensive. Boetsch, Green and Pennington (1996) report convergent results from three samples of dyslexic children and adolescents in which, compared to controls, they perceive themselves as having lower intellectual ability, lower competence in academic skills (reading, writing, spelling and maths) and lower global self worth. The groups did not generally differ on self perceptions of social competence, athletic competence or physical appearance. However, in two out of the three samples the dyslexic group were also lower on behavioural conduct.

Implications for practice

McGuire (1994) concludes her review of the measurement of self concept in children as follows: 'Harter's self perception profiles are currently one of the best measures of children's self evaluations because they are based on a developmental theory of the self. In addition, multiple domains are assessed which are important to children in each age group and self-worth is measured directly. Clinicians may find these scales particularly useful for identifying the areas of competence which influence a child's self worth.' (p.86).

11. Wechsler Intelligence Test for Children: The ACID Profile
Author: D. Wechsler
Publisher: The Psychological Corporation/
Harcourt Brace Jovanovich.
Date of publication: 1992

Description

The procedure for identifying an ACID profile is outlined in the WISC-IIIUK manual (Wechsler, 1992). A student's scores on Arithmetic, Coding, Information and Digit Span are compared to the remaining seven WISC-III subtests, excluding Mazes and Symbol Search. If scores on all 4 (ACID) subtests are equal to or lower than the lowest score on the seven non-ACID subtests, then the pupil is considered to have a positive ACID profile.

Theoretical rationale

The ACID profile was empirically, rather than theoretically derived. However, a number of authors have offered possible interpretations of the higher (although still low) incidence of this profile among dyslexic children. In recent years the likely role of phonological working memory has most frequently been highlighted (Spafford, 1989; Turner, 1997).

Empirical status

Some authors have claimed that the ACID profile is of value in the identification and diagnosis of dyslexia in individuals (Vargo, Grossner & Spafford, 1995). However, while the incidence of the ACID profile, and other related profiles, is found to be higher in SpLD samples than in a random sample of the normal population, the very small differences in population base rates mean that the profiles are not useful in individual assessment. Where conflicting conclusions have appeared, these can generally be shown to be due to inappropriate interpretations of the data. A common source of confusion relates to the extrapolation of conclusions from between group comparisons to conclusions about the diagnostic or educational relevance to individuals. For example, Vargo, Grossner and Spafford's (1995) conclusion about the value of the ACID profile in diagnosis is not valid as the study confines itself to between group comparisons and no individual classification is attempted.

Frederickson (1999) reports the results of the major studies in the last five years which have investigated the use of the ACID profile in the identification of children with SpLD (Dyslexia). These studies successfully address a range of problems for which WISC profile research is frequently criticised: lack of clear specification of subjects, absence of normal control group, wide age ranges and small sample sizes (Miller & Walker, 1981). In addition Greenblatt, Mattis and Trad (1991) point out that most studies involving the ACID profile report on group data rather than individual cases whereas these studies carefully evaluate between group differences on the one hand and utility in individual diagnosis on the other.

Prifitera and Dersch (1993) compared percentage of children with the WISC-III ACID profile from an SpLD sample to the percentages in the standardisation sample. Although the incidence rate of the ACID profile was significantly greater in the SpLD sample than that reported for the normative sample, it was only 5 per cent in the SpLD sample.

Watkins, Kush and Glutting (1997) included all students who received the United States equivalent of a multidisciplinary assessment under Section 323 of the Education Act 1996 in one school year in three south-western suburban school districts in the USA. Classifications were made by multidisciplinary teams using school district criteria consistent with federal and state guidelines. The definition of learning disability (SpLD) included the presence of a significant ability-achievement discrepancy. The incidence of the ACID profile in the SpLD group in this study was only 4.1 per cent.

The discriminative power of the ACID profile in individual diagnosis was investigated by comparing the proportions correctly categorised of the SpLD sample in this study and the WISC-III normative sample. The ACID profile correctly classified only 25 out of the 612 children in the SpLD sample. By contrast 24 children from the normative sample were incorrectly classified as SpLD. On the basis of this study it can be predicted that, were the ACID profile to be introduced as a diagnostic requirement, eligibility for SpLD statements would be cut by 92 per cent! However half the children receiving such statements would not be found by multi-professional assessment to warrant them. Watkins *et al.* (1997) would seem justified in their conclusion that the ACID profile is 'a poor diagnostic indicator'. (p.315).

Watkins, Kush and Glutting (1997) however also consider the possibility that relatively poorer scores on the ACID subtests may be related to performance on academic achievement measures and may therefore still prove to be of some clinical utility. They examined standardised scores on reading, maths and written expression and could find no differences between SpLD children with and without ACID profiles.

Implications for practice

In discussing their findings, Ward, Ward, Hatt, Young and Molner (1995) sum up the current situation well. 'Although the ACID profile was statistically more prevalent in the SpLD group, the low incidence of the profile in the clinical samples renders it clinically meaningless. Therefore, the ACID profile should not be required for diagnosis, nor should the mere absence of the ACID profile be sufficient evidence to relinquish suspicion of a disability.' (p.274).

12. Wilkins Rate of Reading Test
Authors: A.J. Wilkins, R.J. Jeanes, P.D. Pumfrey & M. Laskier
Publisher: I.O.O. Marketing Ltd. (Fund raising for the Institute of Optometry)
Date of publication: 1996

Description

The test is designed to assess the effects of optometric intervention. It consists of lists of 15 high frequency English words presented in a random order. Visually the lists look like four passages. In line with the theory of visual discomfort (see below), the typeface is very small with closely spaced lines and letters. Two passages are read when covered by a preferred coloured overlay, two without. Calculations of the number of words read correctly per minute enable comparisons to be made between the two conditions.

Theoretical rationale

A theory of visual discomfort or stress provides the rationale for the test (see Section 4.8).

It is based on the observation that certain patterns of stripes can induce seizures in individuals with photosensitive epilepsy, photophobia in those with migraine, and perceptual distortion in children with reading difficulty, many of whom have migraine in the family (see Wilkins *et al.*, 1996 for references to the research). The main purpose of the test is to measure whether coloured lenses or overlays have a beneficial effect for individuals with eye strain, headaches, photosensitive epilepsy or reading difficulties.

Empirical status

Research reported by Wilkins *et al.* (1996) shows that performance on the test is reliable on retest but not strongly correlated with age or with performance on conventional reading tests. A substantial number of the sample of children aged 8-11 read faster with the assistance of overlays. As they did not have reading difficulties, the relevance of the test is not dependent on the identification of dyslexia but on signs of visual discomfort when reading.

Implications for practice

Optometrists will find this test useful in enabling them to compare an individual's performance under different visual conditions. It should be noted, however, that the test provides no normative data about rate of reading.

APPENDIX C REFERENCES

Bear, G.G., Clever, A., & Proctor, W.A. (1991). Self perceptions of nonhandicapped children and children with learning disabilities in integrated classes. *Journal of Special Education, 24,* 4, 409-426.

Bedi, G.C. (1994). Low levels of visual and auditory processing in dyslexic readers. City University of New York, USA: *Unpublished PhD thesis.*

Boetsch, E.A., Green, P.A., & Pennington, B.F. (1996) Psychosocial correlates of dyslexia across the life span. Development and Psychopathology, 8, 539-562.

Fawcett, A. & Nicolson,R. (1996) *The Dyslexia Screening Test (D.S.T.).* London: The Psychological Corporation.

Fawcett, A., Nicolson, R. & Dean, P. (1996). Impaired performance of children with dyslexia on a range of cerebellar tasks. *Annals of Dyslexia, 46,* 259-283.

Frederickson, N. (1999). The ACID test – or is it? *Educational Psychology in Practice, 15,* 1, 2-8.

Frederickson, N. & Wilson, J. (1996). Phonological awareness training: A new approach to phonics teaching. *Dyslexia, 2,* 101-120.

Frith, U. (1995). Dyslexia: Can we have a shared theoretical framework? *Educational and Child Psychology, 12,* 1, 2-11.

Gathercole, S.E., Willis, C., Baddeley, A.D. & Emslie, H. (1994). The Children's Test of Nonword Repetition: A test of phonological working memory. *Memory, 2,* 103-127.

Greenblatt, E., Mattis, S. & Trad, P.V. (1991). The ACID pattern and the freedom from distractibility factor in a child psychiatric population. *Developmental Neuropsychology, 7,* 121-130.

McDougall, S., Hulme, C., Ellis, A.W. & Monk, A. (1994). Learning to read: the role of short-term memory and phonological skills. *Journal of Experimental Child Psychology, 58,* 112-133.

McGhee, R. (1996). Formal Assessment. In G. Reed (Ed.) *Dimensions of Dyslexia.* Edinburgh: Moray House Publications.

McGuire, S. (1994). Measuring self-concept in children. *Association for Child Psychology and Psychiatry Newsletter, 16, 2,* 83-87.

Miles, T.R. (1993). *Dyslexia: The Pattern of Difficulties (Second Edition).* London: Whurr.

Miller, N.L. (1994). A neuro-psychological exploration of the Boder Test of Reading-Spelling Patterns. Kent State University, USA: *Unpublished PhD thesis.*

Miller, M. & Walker, K. (1981). The myth of the LD WISC-R profile. *Exceptional Children, 28,* 83-88.

Newton, M.J. & Thompson, M.E. (1979a). Towards early diagnosis of dyslexia. In M.J. Newton, M.E. Thompson & I.L. Richards (Eds.) (1979) *Readings in Dyslexia.* Wisbeach: Learning Development Aids.

Newton, M.J. & Thompson, M.E. (1979b). A concurrent validity study on the Aston Index. In M.J. Newton, M.E. Thompson & I.L. Richards (Eds.) (1979) *Readings in Dyslexia.* Wisbeach: Learning Development Aids.

Newton, M.J. & Thompson, M.E. & Richards, I.L. (1979). The Aston Index as a predictor of written language difficulties: A longitudinal study. In M.J. Newton, M.E. Thompson & I.L. Richards (Eds.) (1979) *Readings in Dyslexia.* Wisbeach: Learning Development Aids.

Nicolson, R. (1996). Developmental dyslexia : past, present and future. *Dyslexia, 2,* 190-207.

Nicolson, R. & Fawcett, A. (1990). Automaticity : A new framework for dyslexia research? *Cognition, 30,* 159-182.

Nicolson, R. & Fawcett, A. (1994). Reaction times and dyslexia. *Quarterly Journal of Experimental Psychology, 47A,* 29-48.

Nicolson, R. & Fawcett, A. (1995). Dyslexia is more than a phonological disability. *Dyslexia, 1,* 19-36.

Nicolson, R., Fawcett, A. & Dean, P. (1995). Time estimation deficits in developmental dyslexia: evidence for cerebellar involvement. *Proceedings of the Royal Society of London: Biological Sciences, 259,* 43-47.

Nockleby, D.M. & Galbraith, G.G. (1984). Developmental dyslexia subtypes and the Boder Test of Reading-Spelling Patterns. *Journal of Psycho-Educational Assessment, 2,* 91-100.

Prifitera, A. & Dersch, J. (1993). Base rates of WISC-III diagnostic subtest patterns among normal, learning disabled, and ADHD samples. *Journal of Psychoeducational Assessment, WISC-III Monograph,* 43-55.

Pumfrey, P.D. (1985). *Reading Tests and Assessment Techniques. (Second Edition).* London: Hodder & Stoughton.

Rack, J., Snowling, M. & Olson, R.K. (1992). The nonword reading deficit in developmental dyslexia: A review. *Reading Research Quarterly, 27,* 29-53.

Reason, R. (1984). The Boder Test of Reading-Spelling Patterns. In P.Levy & H. Goldstein (Eds.) *Tests in Education: A Book of Critical Reviews.* London: Academic Press.

Reynolds, C.R. (1986). Clinical acumen but psychometric naivete in neuro-psychological assessment of educational disorders. *Archives of Clinical Neuropsychology, 1,* 121-137.

Spafford, S. (1989). Weschler digit span subtest: Diagnostic usefulness with dyslexic children. *Perceptual and Motor Skills, 69,* 115-125.

Snowling, M. (1995). Phonological processing and developmental dyslexia. *Journal of Research in Reading, 18,* 132-138.

Stackhouse, J. & Wells, B. (1997). How do speech and language problems affect literacy development. In C. Hulme & M. Snowling (Eds.) *Dyslexia: Biology, Cognition and Intervention*. London: Whurr.

Stanovich, K.E., Siegel, L.S., Gottardo, A., Chiappe, P. & Sidhu, R. (1997). Subtypes of developmental dyslexia: Differences in phonological and orthographic coding. In B.A. Blachman (Ed.) *Foundations of Reading Acquisition and Dyslexia: Implications for Early Intervention*. Mahwah, NJ, USA: Lawrence Erlbaum Associates.

Sutherland, M.J. & Smith, C.D. (1991). Assessing literacy problems in mainstream schooling: A critique of three literacy screening tests. *Educational Review, 43*, 1, 39-48.

Thomson, M. (1975). Laterality and reading attainment. *British Journal of Educational Psychology, 45*, 317-321.

Turner, M. (1995). The Dyslexia Institute, Staines, England. Personal communication with S. Gathercole.

Turner, M. (1997). *Psychological Assessment of Dyslexia*. London: Whurr.

Van-den-Bos, K.P. (1984). Letter processing in dyslexic subgroups. *Annals of Dyslexia, 34*, 179-193.

Vargo, F.E., Grossner, G.S. & Spafford, C.S. (1995). Digit span and other WISC-R scores in the diagnosis of dyslexic children. *Perceptual and Motor Skills, 80*, 1219-1229.

Ward, S.B., Ward, T.J., Hatt, C.V., Young, D.L. & Molner, N.R. (1995). The incidence and utility of the ACID, ACIDS, and SCAD profiles in a referred population. *Psychology in the Schools, 32*, 267-276.

Watkins, M.W., Kush, J.C. & Glutting, J.J. (1997). Discriminant and predictive validity of the WISC-III ACID profile among children with learning disabilities. *Psychology in the Schools, 34*, 4, 309-319.

Weschler, D. (1992). *Weschler Intelligence Scale for Children – Third Edition UK: Manual*. Sidcup, Kent: The Psychological Corporation/Harcourt Brace Jovanovich.

Wilkins, A., Jeanes, R.J., Pumfrey, P.D. & Laskier, M. (1996). Rate of reading test: its reliability, and its validity in the assessment of the effects of coloured overlays. *Ophthalmic and Physiological Optics, 16*, 6, 491-497.

Appendix D:
A FRAMEWORK FOR PSYCHOLOGICAL ASSESSMENT AND INTERVENTION
Adapted from the *DECP Newsletter* – February 1999

The framework has been drafted by the DECP and incorporates comments from clinical psychologists who work with children and young people. It is suggested that it is read in conjunction with the *DECP Guidelines for the Practice of Professional Educational Psychologists* (1993).

The framework is particularly timely given the challenging assumptions about educational psychologists' practice in the media and education, and the need for greater accountability. Its purpose is to recognise that, although psychological assessment is a highly individualised, complex and creative process, there are some fundamental underpinning principles relevant to all educational psychologists.

The framework is intended to guide assessments by educational psychologists which are undertaken at any stage of the Code of Practice (DfEE, 1994). It emphasises the direct link between assessment and intervention and assumes a number of activities within the process of assessment: the assessment activity, the intervention and the written recording and reporting.

PSYCHOLOGICAL ASSESSMENT

Psychological assessment of children and young people has moved beyond the positivist and reductionist frameworks that, for many years, dominated psychological thinking. Current models of assessment need to reflect the body of psychological knowledge, which emphasises the dynamic, interactive nature of children's learning and social behaviours within the environments in which they develop.

A psychological assessment involves the use of a variety of tools, techniques and approaches that draw on relevant psychological theory and research. The purpose of the assessment is to generate understanding of what is happening, who is concerned, why it is a problem and what can be done to make a difference to the situation.

Assessment of children and young people seeks to provide information on the processes of learning, the young person's cognition, social and emotional development and the impact of the context on those areas.

A useful summary of the purpose of psychological assessment was composed by Frederickson *et al.* in 1991:

'We believe that psychological assessments should involve a creative investigation of a broad range of hypotheses that builds on research from all areas of psychology.'

PRINCIPLES OF EDUCATIONAL PSYCHOLOGICAL ASSESSMENT

1. Assessment techniques and models are based on an understanding of current psychological theories and research.

2. Assessment techniques and materials are selected on the basis of:

+ relevance to the presenting problem and to the purpose of the assessment (for example, to address concerns about a child's or young person's learning or behaviour, to monitor progress, for purposes of accountability);

+ sensitivity to ethnic, linguistic, and cultural background as well as the emotional and developmental levels of the child or young person;

+ when psychometric or standardised measures are used, these should be used with reference to their reliability, validity and possible bias. Any references made should be based on an appreciation of the statistical properties of the instrument and detail how these have been derived from the data;

+ positive steps will be taken to avoid bias in the process of assessment.

3. Assessment acknowledges that children and young people develop as a result of an interaction between themselves and their environment.

   Assessment will, therefore:

+ be conducted over time and in relation to different contexts;

+ be formative and provide the necessary results to inform any required intervention;

+ involve parents and/or carers as essential contributors to the process;

+ consider the young person's strengths and difficulties, and generate a number of hypotheses that consider the range of issues;

+ have a possible impact on learning, social or emotional development;

+ incorporate the child's understanding of his or her world;

+ draw, where appropriate, on the views of other professionals.

4. Educational and child psychologists will be aware of the impact of their own belief systems and attitudes on assessment practice. These should be based on sound psychological principles and focused upon solutions rather than problems.

5. Educational and child psychologists will be aware of and acknowledge the impact of assessment processes and activities on:

+ the child or young person, e.g. self esteem, self perception, motivation;

+ the family, e.g. expectations of the child;

+ the school system, e.g. curriculum, teaching and learning, and expectations.

6. The reporting of assessment outcomes. Data should be sensitively presented and relate to the purpose of the assessment.

7. Assessment practice is informed by continuing professional development.

8. Assessment practice will conform to The British Psychological Society *Code of Conduct, Ethical Principles and Guidelines*.

A MODEL OF ASSESSMENT

- The model has been constructed to illustrate the practice described in the text; a framework for the psychological assessment of children, that can with elaboration describe assessment in a range of settings.

- Applied psychology is at the centre of informing the chosen assessment method with the assessment process providing the motive force.

- Psychological assessment is embedded in a context and takes place in a climate sensitive to ethical practice, equality of opportunity, politics and values.

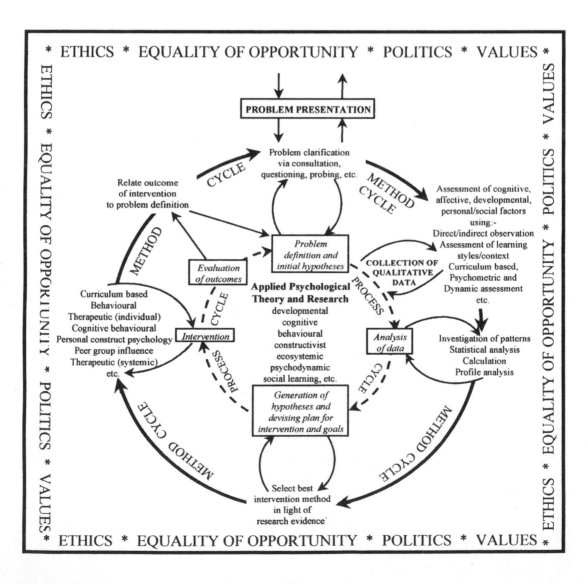